Henry Woodd Nevinson

In the Valley of Tophet

Henry Woodd Nevinson

In the Valley of Tophet

ISBN/EAN: 9783744742542

Printed in Europe, USA, Canada, Australia, Japan

Cover: Foto ©Lupo / pixelio.de

More available books at **www.hansebooks.com**

IN THE VALLEY OF TOPHET

BY

HENRY W. NEVINSON
AUTHOR OF "NEIGHBOURS OF OURS"

"*The Cause of the Poor in God's name and the Devil's!*"
CARLYLE.

LONDON
J. M. DENT AND CO.
1896

Printed by BALLANTYNE, HANSON & CO.
At the Ballantyne Press

CONTENTS

CHAP.		PAGE
I.	A VICARIOUS SACRIFICE	1
II.	AN UNDESIRED VICTORY	21
III.	THE TALE OF SHADOW	39
IV.	ON THE ROAD TO PARNASSUS	58
V.	HIS EWE LAMB	75
VI.	AN ANTI-SOCIAL OFFENDER	94
VII.	THE OLD ADAM	120
VIII.	AN AUTUMN CROCUS	138
IX.	MISS RACHEL	164
X.	THE TRAGEDY OF KINESTEAD	190
XI.	GEORDIE'S MARROW	226
XII.	AN OLD RED RAG	250

IN THE VALLEY OF TOPHET

I

A VICARIOUS SACRIFICE

ALL the village agreed that there was something queer and unholy about Mother Gough. Her cottage with the little workshed at its side was the last along the hill, and the children, on their way to the few starved fields and naked refuse-heaps which did duty for country amongst the pits, crossed the black road before they came to it, and hurried past with furtive glances at the grim old figure standing there, half revealed by the orange light of her furnace, as with one hand she plied the bellows, and with the other plunged the ends of thin iron rods into the burning "gleeds."

It was a land of iron and fire—a land where nature and man seemed to have combined to make a desolation and call it wealth. Over the whole face of it lights and furnaces winked and flared. By day the columns of smoke rose blue and white and black from the plain; by night they reflected the dusky glare of flames. Iron and coal and serviceable marl were there, lying in layers within the common bed of earth. And on the distracted surface dwelt a race of men accustomed for generations to work the coal for great towns and distant countries, and with skilled hands to beat the iron and mould the clay into every shape and use. They were certainly not a people to be alarmed at any earthly purpose to which fire might be put, and every one knew that Mother Gough had done nothing from her girlhood but forge nails from morning to night. But still the late marketers coming home to Wenley-on-the-Hill never felt quite comfortable at the sight of the sparks flying up from her workshop's chimney, and as they went by they would whistle or laugh to drown the clink of her tiny anvil, till they came to the welcome gas-lamp which marked the beginning of the long village street.

And there were stranger sounds to be heard

than the beating of the anvil. At times her voice came issuing from the shed as though in vehement entreaty. It was like a stern warrior pleading for the life of some one he loved. But no one ever heard a voice that answered. Some said she was praying, but prayer of such impassioned wildness had never been known in that country. Prayer was a thing of hassocked knees and Sabbath intonation. It could not be prayer she uttered. Perhaps she only addressed her ravings to a few old fowls which roosted on the smoky rafters of the shed, and peered down out of the darkness, their glittering eyes alone visible. It might be so; she was certainly mad. But more mysterious rumours were whispered up and down. Unimaginative as the people were, their early superstitions of witch and devil died but slowly. "She's carryin' on with sperrits," they said; and it was remembered that Mother Gough had once lived like other folk, and was a respectable widow in high repute for cleanliness and sanctity, as widows surely ought to be. No one had been more regular at the New Connexion chapel, and as, with her beautiful girl at her side, she sat gazing at the preacher whilst he discoursed on atonement and vicarious sacrifice, she would have made a picture for a tract on contented and God-fearing poverty. But suddenly there was a change. It came within a year after her daughter went to service in Birmingham, and died there, or at any rate disappeared. The widow was seen no more at any place of Sunday worship. She shut her door against the kindly gossip. To avoid her old acquaintance, she waited till after sunset on Saturdays before starting to carry her bag of nails to the Netherton fogger (sweater) for whom she worked, and it was late at night when she returned with her bundle of iron rods for the next week's labour. One early morning a Bible was found sticking in the withered hedge opposite her door, its leaves drooping at random like the wings of a shot pigeon. Her name was in it, and they brought it back. She threw it on the furnace and stirred it deep down into the coals. Then the village knew for certain that Mother Gough had sold herself to the powers of evil. Fred Willow of the Bull's Head was the only man who absolutely denied it.

"Even females," he said, "don't sell themselves for nothing. And what's she got to show in return? There's not a body in these parts works 'arder nor lives poorer."

But the strangest thing of all was that Mother Gough herself believed in the compact more firmly than any one. She had deliberately bargained herself away, body and soul, for ever; and she alone knew the price which was being paid her in return.

The years brought no change in her unblest and lonely days. But people became accustomed to her mystery, and rather liked to reflect on her existence as adding a certain importance to their village. It was pleasant to sink the voice and look apprehensively round when the tale had to be told again to some wondering stranger in the taproom. It was not every village which could point to an actual testimony of the Evil One's presence and power. Ordinary wickedness and crime were far too common to be taken as conclusive evidence. But Wenley-on-the-Hill could put in a claim to something more definite than that, one was proud to say.

At last there came a night in early March, when the long frost had relaxed its hold upon the land, and the snowdrifts lay blackened and slowly melting along the edges of the heavy lanes. The wind came rushing from the west with boisterous and refreshing vigour. Over a line of far-off hills the shapeless waning moon had risen late and dim as a ghost. Lights still flickered below in the wide valley of pits and swarming towns. The faint panting of engines could be heard in the distance. But the public-houses in Wenley were closed, and the few fathers of families who could afford a glass so late in the week as Friday night had tramped homeward, leaving in the street a silence that could be felt—a silence intensified rather than broken because one could just hear that at the far end of the village, outside the comradeship of the sleeping homes, Mother Gough was still at work with hammer and hissing forge. She stood in the firelight, her mouth tight set, her thin arms and shoulders bare, working on from hour to hour with no apparent effort or variation. Fifteen blows on the stiddy, a sharp cut across the hardy's edge, a few taps on the head of the iron as it lay in the bore, a jerk with the whimsey, and out leapt the glowing nail. And before it could cool, another lay glowing at its side. So the work had gone on since early morning, the woman-machine of life and blood never flinching nor dealing one false blow. The bellows sighed; the white flame spouted up crackling; the fowls blinked at it and slept. All the country-side slept but for her — but for her and a handful of men on night-shift grubbing in a coal-mine a thousand feet below her forge.

"Mother," said a sweet and musical voice outside the door. The woman looked sidelong and shivered, but paid no other heed.

"Mother," came the call again.

The nail was jerked out crooked from the bore. It was the first crooked nail that day. She took it in the pincers, beat it straight upon the stiddy, and drew another rod white-hot from the blast.

The door opened. In rushed the impetuous wind, scattering the coal-dust, and making the fowls flutter and exclaim indignantly on their perch. A tall figure entered, and a sweet, pale face looked out from the muffling of a fur-lined cloak. Then the door was shut again. But the old woman never turned her head.

"Mother, I've come back to you at last. Don't you know me?" said the voice.

"Ay," muttered the widow to herself; "I know thee right enough. Thee be'st mostly standin' there and callin'. But I did 'ope I'd get through to-night without thee comin'."

"Oh, don't speak like that. Look at me, mother. I'm the only one that ever called you that."

"Oh yes, I know thee," said the old woman again, working the hammer still, but faltering in the strokes. "And I know who they be that send thee to frighten an old sinner so as they may grab her the sooner. But you go back and tell them I've got used to it, and make no account of sperrits now. They'd best try some other way."

"Mother, I've come back to you," said the voice, with calm persistence.

"Don't keep on worritin'," answered the ghost-ridden old woman, though she trembled all over. "Get down into the gleeds same as usual, and leave me to finish my stent. And you may tell them as send thee I'll keep my contrack right enough without them drivin' young females out into the dark at this time of night. It ain't decent for females to be about the streets, not though they're nothink only sperrits." She tried to laugh, but the laugh ended in a moan.

"Don't talk like that, mother," said the voice pleadingly. But the old woman's mouth was more tightly set, and her wrinkled face looked grim, as though defying the arch-enemy to do his worst. She went on with her hammering, and one after another the hot nails fell on to the little heap, and turned from red to grey.

A white hand, with a glittering ring on it, was laid upon her arm. Instantly hammer and rods fell clashing down on the red brick floor. Her body grew rigid. Her eyes were fixed upon the blank darkness which hid the opposite wall. "It's coom at last," she said. "My hour is coom."

"Mother," said the voice, "it's me. Look. I've come to fetch you away."

The old woman shuddered with terror. "I know, I know," she said; "it's the end of the contrack. I did somehow 'ope it wasn't coomin' yet awhile. But it's all right. I'll pay—I'll pay up fair."

"O mother," cried the voice, "don't talk. Only look at me." The other white hand was laid upon the withered cheek, and drew the reluctant head very gently round. At last they looked in each other's faces.

"Mother," said the one again.

"Jenny!" cried the stern old witch, and they fell into each other's arms.

Then followed soft little feminine sounds of consolation, and the old woman laid her head against her daughter's breast, and cried like a child which in its mother's embrace recovers from the terrors of darkness.

"O Jenny, Jenny!" she sobbed, "I never knowed it was theeself. Forgive an old body as lives mostly with queer things as coom and go. I can't believe it's really thee. But oh, it's a sweet comfort to see thee somehow changed. Till now you've always coom same as you was, and stood and called."

"There, mother, there," the daughter said, stroking the thick grey hair. "Of course I've changed. Think how many years it is. There's nothing of a spirit about me. Spirits don't grow older, you know. And that must be very nice for them too," she added, with a little low laugh in which a sigh was mingled.

"It's thee, Jenny—it's really thee," said the mother, looking up. "I scarce believe it. But coom into the cottage, and I'll give thee to eat, and set thee to bed."

The daughter flung half of her great cloak round the old woman like a wing, and together they passed through the midnight wind to the little cottage door.

"That's the smell of the old scented geranium," said Jenny as they entered.

"No, it ain't the old 'un. It's the child of that. The old 'un faded and got burnt in the fire. But there'll be rain, I doubt. Her always smells sweetest afore the rain, same as most things are best afore ill luck. It's a prophecy."

With tremulous eagerness she began to set out the bread and two broken mugs on the table. Jenny's cloak slid from her shoulders as softly as water, and revealed the rich, soft dress beneath. She stood by the fire spreading out her long white hands to the warmth. The jewels flashed in her rings. She seemed some gracious queen of faery sheltering in a witch's hut. As she looked round at the unchanged and desolate old home, with its cheap scraps of decoration, and its fading photographs, more faded now, the remembrance of poverty came over her, and she shivered.

"Now, dear," said her mother, "coom and take a drop of tea to keep out the cold. And I'll go and put this hot brick in your bed. It's all ready, just as it stood the very day as thee left it. And in the mornin' I'll set the brown basin in the scullery by the coals for to wash thee in, same as you'd used to."

Jenny shivered again, and her eyes were full of pity when the old woman returned, and looking up lovingly, took her hands in hers to chafe them warm. The old face was like a rock in sunshine.

"Never mind about all those things now," Jenny said. "I'm hungry; but we won't go to bed to-night. We've got too much to say. And it's so sweet to see you again."

"It's good of thee to speak it, Jenny, but what it is to me passes sayin'," the mother answered.

After the scanty meal they settled themselves in front of the fire, and remained together whilst the hours of night went slowly on.

Jenny curled herself up on the hearthrug, with her head propped against her mother's knees. Sometimes she slept a little; sometimes she sang wild love-songs very softly to herself, as though for pure joy of heart; sometimes she poured out a long and musical sequence of endearing words whilst she kissed the hard and worn old hands. Every movement told of grace and tenderness. Her spirit seemed to overflow with love, with a passionate desire to win more pleasure for herself by making another share in her own abundant happiness. The mother for the most part sat silent, and gazed down on the rich brown hair, as though she hardly ventured yet to realise the unaccustomed joy. Or if she spoke, it was but a few solemn words of love in return for a caress; or she answered some common question of daily life, or spoke of her work, or of the neighbours of long ago, just as if nothing had happened between, and Jenny had never ventured beyond the village school. In the unreality of those early hours before the dawn, it would not have been hard to persuade her that the haunted interval of sacrifice and pain had also been unreal. She dwelt in a bewildered Paradise.

"Mother," said Jenny at last, sitting up and counting the strokes as the village clock struck four, "we must be moving now. I must be away by five."

"What's that thee says?" asked the old woman indifferently, as one speaks in dreams.

"I must catch the very first train at Old Hill Station, and it's a long way to walk. Oh, I've planned it all out. You see, I must be at rehearsal to-morrow afternoon. They can't get on without me. I'm famous now," she added, with a low but joyous laugh; "and I have to pay for fame."

"I've paid all I could. It ain't right for 'er to pay as well," said the mother to herself.

"Besides," Jenny went on, throwing her head back with another smile, "I promised my husband to be with him again to-morrow."

The mother suddenly sat up straight, drawing in her breath, and looked down on the happy face with the sorrow of some ancient goddess of destiny. "Which 'oosband, ye poor Samarian woman?" she said.

Jenny rose up, and stood with folded hands, looking at the smouldering fire. "Now, mother," she said simply, "you must not be hard on me. I don't feel particularly wicked. I never did."

"That's blessed hearin'," said the mother, with a sigh.

"I always said to myself I'd come and see you if I got married. Well, I was married last week. My husband's a true man. I must go back to him now—to him and the play. That comes of being famous." She laughed again. In truth, she was very well thought of in London as the heroine in refined and graceful comedy.

"I don't know nothink about bein' famous. But oh, I did 'ope thee had coom back to stop," said the old woman, and put her hands before her face.

Kneeling at her side, Jenny drew them softly away, and laid her cheek where they had been.

"Why, mother," she said, "I've come to take you away with me. I told you so. Come now, this minute. We'll soon put your things together."

She sprang up, and moved swiftly about, choosing the few old possessions she thought her mother might like to take with her. When she had folded them all up in a white apron, the bundle was small enough. The old woman watched her helplessly without a word. She was dazed and bewildered at the idea of departure. The whole thing seemed to be no concern of hers. And yet the thought kept coming: "To go, to escape, to be rid of it all—oh, it would be an immortal mercy!"

She suffered herself to be dressed in bonnet and shawl. "Now, mother," cried Jenny, seizing the bundle, "we're off;" and she flung the door wide open. In the west the night was still dark, but the church and houses down the village street showed pale and grey in the first glimmer of morning.

"Quick," said Jenny, "before any one's up. They'll only gossip and speak evil."

"I've never spoke evil of thee, Jenny—never once."

"I'm sure you haven't, dear. But quick, say good-bye to the old forge for ever and ever. Oh, I'm so happy."

"For ever and ever," said the mother, but did not move from the doorway. Her face was stern again with set resolve as at the first. "It's good-bye to thee, Jenny," she said. "I can't never coom with thee. I'm under a contrack for ever and ever."

"O mother, what does a contract matter? We'll soon pay that off. Quick, come along!"

"Never no further, Jenny. Them as the contrack's with don't take no money. It's no good you draggin' at me. It ain't to be."

"Now you must really not talk nonsense, mother. Give me your arm."

"Good-bye, Jenny darlin'," said the mother. "Kiss me once more."

"Oh, what am I to do?" cried Jenny. "Come with me, do come, just to please your little Jenny!" She stooped and smiled down on her, holding the withered old chin in the cup of her hand, as she sometimes did to a lover on the stage.

Tears came into her eyes; but her mother only shook her head.

"It's no good," she said. "I made the contrack. The other party's actin' fair, as far as I can see, and I ain't the woman to go back on my word. Go now, dear, or thee'll be late. And take back all what thee sent, and send me no more money, dear." She drew from her bosom a blue bag containing a few old notes and postal orders, and tucked it into Jenny's waistband. "But maybe some day thee can coom again just for one minute."

Tears and entreaties were vain. "Good-bye, good-bye. God bless you, mother," Jenny said at last. "I'll often come—as often as my husband and the manager will let me."

She laughed amid tears, and her footsteps sounded lightly down the street. At the bend of the road she turned and waved her hand. The wind blew out her cloak like a sail, and she was gone.

When the sun rose, Mother Gough was still standing at the open door and looking at the point where that figure had vanished. She was muttering words at random to herself: "Jenny said, 'God bless you, mother,' and she said, 'I don't feel particularly wicked. I never did.' 'Cos why? I've took the wickedness on myself so as she shouldn't. And now I know as them who agreed to reckon my old body and soul in place of hern is keepin' their contrack fine. And you may be sure," she cried, stretching her scarred and withered arms out towards the rising sun like an enchantress—"you may be sure I'll never shirk my part on it, neither here nor yet hereafter. I swear, I swear it."

It was dreary to turn back into the cottage, and untie the bundle, and take the warm brick out of the narrow white bed. But as she entered her forge again, and kindled up the little furnace, she felt like one who has at last escaped from a haunted room into the sweet sunshine. She finished her due weight of nails, and before mid-day the Dudley marketers were astonished to find her trudging along with her heavy little sack.

"Twelve pounds and two-quarters," said the fogger, as he weighed it out at the counter of his "tommy-truck" shop. "Well, Mrs. Gough, 'ere's three and tenpence 'alfpenny for the lot, but I can't give yer no more iron. You know very well why."

"Then I'll take fivepence out in bacon, please," said the old woman, trembling at the thought of losing her work.

"That ain't enough," said the fogger.

"Then give me sixpenn'orth of tea beside, please, sir."

He flung the groceries and a bundle of iron rods to her, and as she crept out, he laughed and said to his wife : " Tea ? Carpet-sweepin's and dust was what I give 'er. That's *my* way of doin' business with the devil and all 'is works."

"Quite right too," said his wife. "But did yer notice her was kind of different this mornin' ? I reckon her's been drinkin'."

II

AN UNDESIRED VICTORY

"Give me that shillin'," said Martha Grant.

It was the evening of Palm Sunday now, and she had been repeating this sentence at brief intervals ever since her husband's return from work on Saturday afternoon. Out of the sixteen shillings which Peter earned for working the Wenley "rag" in the quarries, she considered herself entitled to fourteen for keeping house. As to the other two shillings, she had never raised a question; the brutish male must be allowed some margin for his pleasures. But this week he had taken three shillings, and given her but thirteen. That was intolerable.

"Give me that shillin'," she said again, as they reached the doctor's door.

"Look 'ere," he answered at last, breaking a silence which he had preserved unmoved for twenty-four hours, for indeed he was a man of equable temperament and few words—" I ain't goin' to give yer that shillin'; but I'll tell yer what I'll do instead—the very moment as this affair is over, I'll flay yer alive."

"Do it, do it, yer great coward," Martha answered, drawing a grey shawl tighter round her baby. "I don't care nothing about that. You give me that shillin'." And she followed her husband into the doctor's house.

The doctor, though already well advanced into middle age, was a new arrival at Wenley-on-the-Hill. He had come, no one quite knew why, from a London suburb which prided itself on its patronage of intellectual things. His circle of acquaintance there had talked a great deal about painters and the Buddha, had listened to each other's dramas, had kept a trustful look-out for the apparitions of cats and relatives, and had dutifully discussed the magazines every month. They had also established at least two centres for lectures, and had bound themselves into a kind of church for the worship of Ethical Culture—a method of diffusing the highest morality without the aid of superstition. In this society the doctor had represented science — science apart from its supposed harshness and inhumanity, as he would hasten to explain. For indeed he was the gentlest of men, an excellent doctor, a better philosopher, and a better Socialist still.

To a man of such wide intellectual interests the change from the suburb to Wenley was more than lamentable; it was bewildering. It obliterated the landmarks of life. In Wenley, intellect appeared to be an unknown quantity, and its interests were represented by the local *Weekly Advertiser.* No one had even heard of the subjects which had occupied the cultivated leisure of the doctor and his friends. It is true that there had been some talk of erecting a public library within reach of Wenley and a few other pit villages, but the great landowner had put an end to all such hope, by announcing that if people wanted mental luxuries he should be obliged to raise the rents. Once upon a time also a gentleman from London had expounded the geology of the district in a schoolroom a few miles away, and the "doggies" (under-managers) of the Wenley pits still delighted in talking that lecture over with the doctor when he came to their wives' confinements. It seemed to give their country a scientific importance, and to show that they too were not entirely excluded from the freemasonry of mind. But the doctor himself would sigh as he listened, and reflect on the surfeit of that suburb where so many of his friends had earned a precarious enlightenment by taking in each other's lectures.

At last Jeremiah Wilson, an excellent pikeman, turned teetotaller, and went mad from sitting at home in the evenings with his wife and staring at the fire. In sheer terror of insanity the village rushed into drink with greater zeal than ever, and then it was that the doctor set about a new experiment. He fitted up a long low room in his own house with stoves and seats. On the walls he pasted a few sentences of good advice, and hung a photograph of Florence and a carefully prepared skeleton of a toad. This was to be the new shrine of Ethical Culture *in partibus infidelium*. Early in the autumn after his arrival, he opened it on Sunday evenings for lectures, readings, and friendly discussions. He himself began by reading passages from serious authors, such as Thomas à Kempis, in whose works he was careful to replace the name of

God by the word Humanity. Other subjects followed, and occasionally a Progressive Society in Birmingham sent out one of their number to make a speech on the Law of Population or the Utilisation of Sewage. As long as the weather was warm the doctor provided a drink of oatmeal and water flavoured with lemon. When winter came he supplied cocoa. The average attendance for the one was a man (the doctor's coachman), three women, and a child; for the other it rose to eleven. All went away pleased with themselves for their patience and the favour they had done him, and the entertainments were called the Doctor's Drivels.

But the last lecture had yielded something of sensational interest. The doctor had determined to demonstrate the advantages of virtue by a short series of lectures on human physiology. Unable to produce a human body on the platform, he began by dissecting the corpse of a rabbit. Every man present had coursed rabbits; every woman had cooked them. But somehow at the sight of the surgical instruments snipping the various valves and muscles, the men began to faint, and the girls turned sick. Fearing to lose the entire audience, the doctor let the rabbit alone, and exhibited a diagram of an alcoholic liver, illustrating the evil effects of spirits on the system. Confidence was at once restored, and the subject gained a thrilling personal interest from the whispered reflection that the livers of the two most notorious drunkards in the village looked like that. The doctor was much encouraged by the sympathetic hearing, and promised to continue the theme on the following Sunday, with a diagram of the human heart and lungs and some anatomical slides which he would procure from Birmingham for the occasion.

And now the audience was seated, all huddled close together from a kind of shyness, though there was plenty of room. They numbered nearly fifty, and the doctor's kindly heart rose as he looked at them. His efforts were certainly having a measure of success at last. Some no doubt had come for the warmth, some for the cocoa, some to sit still and let the quiet words pour over them. But a few were drawn by the interest of the subject itself and the hope of possible horrors. In the middle of the front row, his purple face resting on his tremulous hands, sat old Issachar, the more notorious of the two drunkards already mentioned. He had come, as he kept defiantly announcing, to see the liver of old Blowy, his only possible rival in intemperance. Just behind him the Grants had taken their places, side by side as married people should, whilst rage smouldered in their hearts. After his brief outburst at the door, Peter had pretended to be entirely unaware of his wife's existence, though now she had turned up the baby's clothes and thrust its naked feet almost into his lap, partly to irritate him, partly to show how much they wanted socks. A respectful murmur pervaded the benches, as when a drawing-room meeting is to open with prayer, and people of fashion are not quite sure how far etiquette requires them to assume the demeanour customary in church. At regular intervals Martha's voice could be distinguished, doggedly repeating the demand, "You give me that shillin'." Her neighbours looked at each other, and laughed.

On the platform the doctor was busy finishing his preparations with the help of his committee —his coachman, namely, a grey-haired old German moulder, and a tall, pallid youth, who had brought over the selected slides from

Birmingham, where he was a rising member of the Progressive Society. The white sheet was now stretched on its bamboo frame. The circle of yellow light had flickered and disappeared and risen again on it, and everything was ready.

Suddenly the doctor's voice was heard in a cry of anguish: "My goodness!"—it was the very strongest exclamation permitted by Ethical Culture—"they've sent us the wrong slides!"

There was a whispered consultation.

"What *is* to be done?" the doctor was heard saying. "And such a subject, too!—I mean for an audience like this. We should never get them here again. And besides, who is to speak on it! I couldn't. It's really too aggravating!" The doctor had acquired a few little feminine turns of speech in suburban *salons*.

"For me also," said the old German, "it would be not possible to speak on this."

The doctor ruffled his grizzled hair in desperation. "We must do something!" he said. "How would it be if the subject were treated merely as a matter of history, and the slides shown as pretty pictures of it?"

"The historical standpoint is good," said the German.

"What do you think, Mr. Goodman ? Won't you try it ? " said the doctor, appealing to the Progressive.

"Well," said that youth jauntily, "I'm not much of a hand at Sunday-school treats myself, but let's just have a look at the slides."

These unfortunate substitutes for anatomical figures were in fact highly-coloured representations of scenes from the life of Christ. There was nothing in the least historic in their treatment. They abounded in a lifeless symbolism, the real meaning of which has long been forgotten in England. And through a false feeling of respect for the subject, the principal figures had been idealised, till the carpenter's son and his fisher friends resembled a mixture of Roman senators and statuesque athletes.

"Well," said the Progressive, "I don't mind having a try at the thing, just to oblige."

There were few subjects at which he would not have had a try. He had been known to lecture on the same day upon Shelley, Bimetallism, and Oliver Cromwell ; and the triumph was that on each subject he had managed to say much the same thing. For he had the makings of an orator.

The doctor sighed with relief, and retired to the lantern at the back of the room.

"Fellow-citizens," began the young Progressive in his easiest manner, running his eye over the dingy little herd of human creatures before him, "owing to some slip in the arrangements of Providence, if I may be allowed to use that obsolete term, we are compelled to-night to put you off with a subject unfortunately much more familiar to you than your own insides. I suppose there is not one among us who hasn't heard of Christ; but there are many who have never seen the human heart and lungs, such as your good doctor promised to show us, although they are at this moment at work in us all. That's the fine result of our national education falsely so called!"

There was an indignant pause, and the due murmur of sympathetic indignation ran through the people. They had not a notion why.

"But," continued the lecturer, "although the subject may be what the gentlemen of the press call a little off, I'll ask you to listen to it sooner than hurt your good doctor's feelings by walking out. And I don't want you to believe every word I say. I'm not much of a hand at believing myself. Why, I never even believed I grew on a gooseberry bush." (A tardy smile, in which the speaker freely joined.) "But I don't bear any particular spite against people who go on believing things, for we should always remember that we can't all be heirs of all the ages, in the foremost ranks of time."

The heavy, labouring feet shuffled assent. The heavy, labouring brains dimly wondered what on earth the man was talking about. The coachman said, "Hear, hear," to reveal his knowledge of politics. Old Issachar loudly expressed his intention of sitting there for ever till old Blowy's liver came round. Martha said, "Where's that shillin'?" Then the heirs of all the ages were silent again.

The first picture on the screen represented the shepherds with their flocks, and the herald angels appearing in the midnight sky with tidings of great joy. A whisper of admiration passed through the darkened room. The people were delighted with the long and swanlike wings. Divining their thoughts, the lecturer hastened to expose the absurdity of making wings sprout from the shoulder-blades, and easily showed it was a violation of all the analogies of comparative anatomy. In the interests of science the doctor felt bound to give a dubious assent from the distance. But science did not in the least affect the people's notion of what an angel ought to be.

To Peter Grant, it is true, those wings and feathers suggested something much nearer to his heart than angels. They brought before him more vividly the one thought which had been there for nearly a week past—the thought of a certain pigeon, Bobby Brook's pigeon, the likeliest of all the flock. Bobby had promised it to a syndicate of seven, who were to put in three shillings apiece, to be paid down on Monday without fail; for Bobby was in difficulties. Such a pigeon to fly had never been bred in Wenley. At the sight of the angels, Peter went through all its points again—the deep, full breast, the faultless wings, the shapely head and tail, the little eye of brilliant red. In six months' time nothing that flew would stand against that pigeon over a mile course, he knew that well. There was money in it, a pound or two a year at least. And the bird was as good as his already! As he thought of it, he clutched the three shillings in his trouser pocket, making them jingle in his joy.

"You give me that shillin'," said his wife, hearing the sound.

The next picture was the manger at Bethlehem. To maintain the sanctity of the subject, the artist had represented all the cattle standing round as first-prize beasts. The lecturer, with an inconsequent memory of his infant school, pointed out that this showed we should be kind to dumb animals.

Kind certainly, thought Peter. How tenderly he would treat that pigeon if once he really owned a share in it. How carefully he would starve it down to the point at which it would fly quickest home for its feed of Indian corn. How fondly he would encourage its speed by biting its feet just before he flung it loose into the air. He smiled to himself, for he seemed to feel its little pink toes between his teeth. But looking down suddenly, he saw that the pink toes kicking against his waistcoat were only his baby's.

With dramatic instinct the speaker passed

more rapidly over the middle course of the life, in order to dwell upon the scenes which led to its close. Slide steadily followed slide, and at each the doctor trembled. Almost every word the young Progressive uttered was torture to his sensitive and finely-educated nature. He dreaded "superstition," but in his heart he detested mockery even more. What if his unhappy audience went away only infected with the windy questionings which so easily pass for wit with the vulgar, and for criticism with the dull?

He need not have been afraid. Irony and scepticism ran off their minds unheeded as water. As the scenes of that short life passed before them, a strange spirit seemed to grow up and pervade the silent room. Even the lecturer was aware of a certain change, and did not escape its effect. From easy mocking he advanced to patronage, and from patronage of Christ he advanced very nearly to simplicity. It was one of those moments when, from the united spirit of many, each soul in a gathering becomes conscious of a power different from himself and stronger. Men and women sat motionless on the benches, and stared. Worn with labour, twisted, hardened, and deformed, smelling of sweat and their kindred dust, body and soul begrimed and stupefied by excess of toil, their very presence between earth and sky dependent on the multiplied strokes of their arms from day to day, they, in that dimly-lighted room surrounded by the outer darkness, might stand as the emblem and epitome of mankind upon his pale little planet, spinning through the dark abyss of space. Savage as well as hungry, unrestrained as well as overworked, they differed from brutes chiefly in that they were conscious of death, and acquainted with grief and sin. But in the midst of their obscurity flickered a tremulous desire for something which might perhaps almost be called righteousness, and all believed they had some share in it. Not one would from his heart have owned himself utterly abandoned and cast away. Full of fond illusion, each kept some point of honour for his pride. To each his very sins were capable of better names. The drunkard called himself an open-hearted comrade ; brutality looked something like manliness. And now a series of scenes was being presented in symbol before their eyes, as once in actual life before the face of man. And again the faint tremor of an immense hope traversed the partial gloom. Here was the thing they had desired to see, the revelation of that righteousness which so long had tormented and comforted them. Through all the dull disguises of art and tradition, through all the flowing robes and halos and other millinery with which a respectable piety had endeavoured to raise the human truth to a decent social level, they did to some extent contrive to pierce to the heart of that history, so simple and unhappy, so like their own lives, and yet so different in achievement and result.

Peter sat and stared with the rest, strange and uncomfortable feelings at work in his mind. At the scene of the Last Supper those feelings suddenly took form. He ought to give up that pigeon. He instantly set the absurd idea aside; it would be ridiculous, just for the sake of a wife too. Then came the prayer in the Garden. Not even the picture of an angel's hand holding out a fine gold cup from a cloud could altogether obscure the meaning of that scene. The call to give up that pigeon came again into Peter's heart, and

AN UNDESIRED VICTORY 37

with all his strength he resisted it. He was sure that could not be required of him. The final pictures came, the end of all those hopes, the reward of such a life. "It is finished," said the lecturer. A woman began to cry. Peter moved his legs uneasily about, and clutched the shilling tight in his hand. Then the scenes ended. The people drew themselves together, and began to cough, glad of the common human sounds which brought them back to daily life.

Some rhymed moral reflections by an American poet were then sung out of a collection called Ethical Hymns, and the doctor in a few kindly words repeated his apology for the unfortunate mistake in the slides.

"I only hope," he added, "that the parson to whom our anatomical figures have probably been sent by mistake has been able to put them to such good account."

"Yes," said the young Progressive, "I think I made the best of the subject."

"An out-of-the-ordinary folk," meditated old Karl Meyer, the German; "they did listen, they did weep, they did believe all. A seldom folk!"

But Peter and his wife had shuffled out into

the night, and were going home without a word. Peter walked in front, and tried to whistle; but it was no good. He could think of nothing but that faultless pigeon. The agony of the sacrifice was upon him. If it were possible, with what joy he would have escaped from it. They entered their little cottage. Martha held the baby under one arm and turned up the lamp. By its light he glanced at her unhappy and hard-set face. He stood for a moment irresolute. Then drawing his hand from his pocket, he violently struck the table with it, making the lamp-glass rattle.

"Take your damned shillin', then!" he said, and sank on a chair by the fire, exhausted by the vain struggle. The share in that pigeon would never be his.

But Martha carefully put the money in her pocket, tucked the baby into its corner of the big bed, and creeping between her husband's knees, laid her face against his open waistcoat. She had never felt so happy since the day they first kept company.

III

THE TALE OF SHADOW

No doubt at some time in his babyhood Shadow had possessed a canonical name like the rest of the baptized world, and his mother had known it. But it had been so long forgotten now, that if any one had called him by it he would not have answered to the word. Some said he was called Shadow because he evidently was not a solid; some, less logically, because he was of too thin an essence to cast any shadow of his own. Anyhow, it was the name which nature intended for him, for within man's memory he went by no other. He was indeed so fugitive and impalpable of substance that he appeared and vanished noiselessly, like a ghostly visitant, and it was one of the jokes of the Trigger pit to shake hands with him till his thin bones rattled together like a skeleton's knuckles. With the men he enjoyed the popularity of a butt; the women liked him for his invariable cheerfulness, and they took an interest in his solitude, for he happened to be one of the very few unmarried adults in Wenley. So every one had a good word for him; but nobody, except himself, realised how great a heart beat within that fairy-like covering of jointed ivory and woven tissue of gossamer which he called his body. And in fact this greatness of heart, like so many of the finest truths, was founded on fiction. For in his childhood the head-manager of the pit, wishing to console Shadow's mother for the decapitation of her husband by the fall of the cage in the shaft, had flatteringly remarked that the boy's nose was like the Duke of Wellington's. The proud mother had repeated the story to her neighbours in the boy's hearing almost every day till her death, and as he grew up Shadow inevitably took the Duke as his model of life, though he knew nothing about him beyond what he could learn from an account of Waterloo, which pointed the moral of a tract on the use of bad language. He had managed, however, to secure a profile portrait of his hero and prototype, on an advertisement of a local brand of safety matches called "England's Glory." And whenever he looked at that portrait hanging over his squalid bed, he ran his finger slowly up and down his straight little nose, and all his blood throbbed with heroic ardour.

In his dress also he affected the precision and smartness required of a soldier. His little cap was always cocked on one side like a grenadier's. His jacket was buttoned up tight to the throat; and when he went to bed he carefully turned his corduroys inside out, and hung them on the door, with a brick tied to each leg, to prevent them bagging at the knees. He cultivated a military courtesy and a military gait. On his rare holidays he went into Birmingham to see the volunteers drill, and he almost worshipped their fat old sergeant-major, who had once been in the Line, and wore a real medal, more precious in Shadow's eyes than any cross of diamonds. From that sergeant-major's example he acquired his own dignity of carriage, drawing in his back and swelling out his chest, till the Wenley women compared him to a pouter pigeon. But no one shared his secret. No one else perceived in him any military quality beyond an amiable self-conceit. To the unimaginative outside world he was queer old. Shadow the " 'oss-fettler," taken on as a "banksman" at the pit mouth in his boyhood because of his father's disaster, and afterwards promoted to the charge of the ponies down the Near Shaft because he was too fragile for a pikeman. But in his own mind, as he ran the light along the ponies' tails in their rock-hewn stable, and then shut the door on them and the cat, leaving them in the profound darkness of the pit, he felt little less pride than the Commanding Officer of a Cavalry Brigade; and in his dreams beneath his hero's portrait he felt a great deal more.

At seven o'clock one pleasant morning in May, Shadow was standing by the shaft, punctual to time as the Duke of Wellington himself. The pit was not working on Sundays, nor even on night-shift; but the ponies, though they were quite aware of the day of rest, had to be rubbed down, and fed, and generally encouraged to continue their existence the same as usual. Shadow was on the point of giving the signal to the engineman to lower away, when Taffy Griffith came running up, and

THE TALE OF SHADOW 43

muttered that it would save trouble if they went down together. This was unusual, for Griffith was Second-Class Certificated Manager of the Far Shaft; and just because the Near and Far Shafts were within thirty yards of each other, and the workings joined below ground, and formed one and the same pit, there was enmity without quarter between the two shafts and all the workers in them. But of all the Far Shaft men there was none so unpopular in the Near Shaft as Griffith. He was a stern, dark-faced miner, very capable and correct, decent in private life, and a model official at his duties; but the Near Shaft hated him, and his one common bond with humanity appeared to be his scorn of them and all their works. Towards Shadow, a mere "'oss-fettler," he would hardly have deigned even to feel scorn, had he not been uneasily conscious at times that Shadow took a peculiar interest in himself. Shadow seemed to haunt him. He would appear in the most unexpected places. He would flutter from behind a hedge on Sunday evenings as Griffith and his wife were coming home from chapel, would say good-night, and vanish. Once, too, at the crisis of a pitched matrimonial battle, just as Griffith was about to adopt the one argument which women are supposed to understand, he could have sworn he saw Shadow's white face flit past the window. At any rate, he dropped his heavy, clenched fist, and stared in silence. For all these things Griffith hated Shadow with as much hatred as a Second-Class Certificated Manager can decently feel towards one so inferior in the social scale.

Nevertheless, he put up with him that morning, for he had his own reasons for going down the Near Shaft. They got on the cage, gave the signal, and down they rushed together into the darkness, the sides of the shaft just glimmering with water as they sped past.

"Missus and the kids all right?" asked Shadow politely, as the cage came to a standstill with a jerk and a clatter just above the sump, on the surface of which the outer sky was reflected like a little threepenny bit. Griffith answered with an indifferent grunt. Inquiries about his wife irritated him. They seemed to encroach on his own importance.

Shadow took a naked candle, and Griffith a safety-lamp, just for the dignity of the thing, and they trudged along the main gallery in silence till they came to the stable door, and heard the ponies whinny at the first gleam of light and the sound of Shadow's footstep.

"I'm a-coomin', my beauties," he said. "You stand steady and keep your dressin' by the right."

"Leave the 'osses a bit, and come along with me," the Welshman growled. "I reckon old Job'll have cleared out by now. He's always an hour afore anybody else on a Sunday."

Job was the corresponding manager of the Near Shaft, and it was to spy upon his work that Griffith had chosen to come down with Shadow that morning. Every now and then as he went along he gave a short and scornful laugh at the signs of his rival's incapacity.

"It's more like a forest than a mine," he said, pointing to a gallery where the pit-props stood in rows like the columns of some primitive temple. "It's about time old Job was led away to the work'us. You've not got a penn'-orth of faith among yer in this shaft, or you'd trust the roof to stand without all that expense in trees and slabs."

"Faith's well enough," said Shadow, "but

I feel more comfortable for 'avin' good timber under it."

As he spoke they reached a "face," where the pikemen (hewers) were at work on weekdays. In the "thick coal," or thirty-foot seam, the pikemen cut away or "under-go" the coal at the bottom, and the "bondsmen" then blow it down with "shots" or blast-cartridges from above, so that it all falls in a confused heap together. At this point the pikemen had finished their part, and in mere contemptuous curiosity Griffith crept on all fours into the deep hollow they had made. As he went he savagely struck with his fist and shook a small slanting prop or "spurn" which cautious old Job had made them set up in accordance with the law, to secure the roof of their low cavern. Shadow, who was creeping close behind him, caught at his arm. "You leave me alone," Griffith said with a curse. "You Near Shaft men ain't fit to be trusted down a pit no more than babbies."

They were now close in against the virgin rock. Griffith lay down on his back, and with his lamp examined the layer of coal over his face. It was hard, stony-looking stuff in broad slabs—"bat" he scornfully called it, and doubted if the shaft was worth the expense of working at all.

All the time there was a soft little rustle or mutter to be heard, like dry leaves just touched by an autumn wind. It was the coal "creeping" or "stirring," as the miners call it, under the disturbance and change of pressure after so many ages of repose. Both men were too familiar with the sound to pay any attention to it. Shadow was squatting close to the manager's side. He was thinking chiefly of the ponies, but a peculiar feeling of courtesy or protection kept him where he was. Suddenly there was a sharp report, as of something giving way, close behind them.

"What's that?" both cried at once, and each saw that the other had turned deathly pale.

"It's heavin'," said Shadow.

"It's a bump," said Griffith; and Shadow turned his head to look.

He saw the pikemen's little prop or spurn had split right down the middle. It was bending to the right, and very, very slowly, as it seemed, it just curled over like a lily's stem till it nearly touched the ground. The thought of escape just flashed through his mind; he was nearest the entrance. He might perhaps have crept out; there was still time. No one ever knew exactly what motives possessed him, but, without reflecting for another moment, he flung himself lengthways upon the manager, drawing up his knees under him and crouching down so as to cover the head and body as with an arch. Strange thoughts sped across his mind and vanished again. Then came the crash and rush of falling coal. The low cavern disappeared. The lights went out. The two men were buried alive, face to face, in the earth's thick rind.

Instinctively they clung to each other for protection, and listened. A few large blocks fell crashing into the gallery outside. Small fragments kept dribbling and stirring with a mysterious sound, like the movement of clay settling down upon a newly-buried coffin. Dust thickened the air and choked their breathing.

When all was still, Shadow said in a terrified whisper, "Mr. Griffith! are yer dead?"

"Get up, get off me!" gasped the manager. "I'm dyin' of yer weight."

"It ain't me," said Shadow, "it's the pit."

"Get from off me," said Griffith again, and groaned.

"It ain't me, I tell yer," Shadow protested; "there's the Top Slipper and the Lambs and the Tar and the Brazils and the Bottom Foot and the Swan and the Slips and the Patchill Bat, all layin' on top of you besides myself. You ain't reasonable, Mr. Griffith, to be complainin' of my weight."

"Oh, I'm dyin'," murmured Griffith. "Both my legs is pinched."

"And the only mercy is you bain't dead," said Shadow; "and flat as frogs under a roller both on us would be if the bat you was laughin' at hadn't fallen solid and got itself wedged up somehow over my back. And as for yer legs, they ain't nothink to what yer 'ead would look like if the bat or my body was to give."

"My poor legs!" cried Griffith again; and Shadow felt his muscles relax, and his breathing appeared to cease.

"He's goin' off," said Shadow, and he clung to him tighter than ever, as though he could hold the life in the body and prevent its escape through the chinks of the coal. What was he to do? There was a ten-foot wall of fallen

D

"stuff" between them and the gallery. He could not rise an inch, and dared not shift his body, even if he could. The supply of air might give out at any moment. The engine-man would not notice their absence for some hours, and even then a rescue must be slow.

"Mr. Griffith!" he shouted, "you keep on livin', or I'll give yer what for."

There was no sign of answer. He ran the fingers of one hand as hard as he could into the manager's neck, till he felt the body tremble again.

"That's better," he said cheerfully. "Now, Mr. Griffith, you just keep awake. I'll teach you to start dyin'!"

"I can't abear no more," groaned the man.

"And I ain't exactly comfortable placed neither," said Shadow, "but that ain't no cause for you to go on dyin'. We've got to spend a quiet day down here, so we'd best make up our mind to it."

Griffith made no answer, but after a few groans of anguish he seemed to be falling back into unconsciousness.

"This won't do at all. He's startin' of it again," said Shadow to himself, feeling like a doctor whose patient's life is slipping away between his remedies. Then he reflected for a moment, as though hesitating over some decisive but dangerous operation.

"William Griffith," he said at last, in a deep whisper, close to the manager's ear, "I'm a-goin' to tell you a little story, just to pass the time away. If we live you can forget it, and if we die you can't remember, so that's all right. It ain't a long story nor yet a queer, but it's all about a girl called Nellie. Now, I ain't sayin' as her was the same as is now yer wife and the mother of two; but the name was Nellie, and some three or four years back her was in love with a man, and that man warn't you. And him—well, he wasn't to be called an extry big man, but all there was of 'im was just chock-full to the skin with the love of her. So it went on for a month or two —such months them was! Fine blue summer weather, and all the world as sweet as a rose after comin' up out of the pit. And there wasn't no tellin' which of them two was wantin' to get married soonest. And then on a sudden it all comes to a dead stop, and there ain't no sayin' for why; only, the man was a good-

'earted, easy-goin', soldier-like feller, very takin', and clean and smart, so as all the women kep' their one eye on 'im. And if she did find 'im settin' on a stile with his arm round another girl after he'd took 'er to the church, and she'd come out sooner than expected through feelin' a kind of rush of love for 'im—there wasn't no harm ever meant in that. It only came through his havin' a kind of tender feelin' towards all females through bein' so much in love with one. But Nellie never thought of nothink of that sort, but bein' a female 'erself, her just went ragin' mad, and within the month had gone and married a stranger from South Wales or somewheres down your way—a great big, clummery, maulin' creatur', same as our old engine at the pit-head. Are you keepin' lively, Mr. Griffith?"

A groan came in answer.

"That's right," said Shadow; "you stick to it. We're gettin' along fine now. But as I was sayin' in my story, that smart and tidy feller hasn't hardly spoke one word to that girl since the day her was married, but he can't help catchin' a sight on her now and then, and he ain't in no sort of a hurry, but every mornin' when that man gets up, and every evenin' when he goes to bed, his one hope is as some day her will be left a widder and give 'im one more chance through her present 'oosband meetin' with an accident. Are yer feelin' any easier, Mr. Griffith?"

There was no answer.

"Oh, confound the gaffer!" said Shadow. "If he ain't goin' off again! Look 'ere, Mr. Griffith, if you keep goin' asleep, I'll 'ave to keep wakin' of yer up. And there's one more point to tell about that story: that 'oosband thinks he's got possession of Nellie, but it's only for a say-so, mind. Nellie's that other man's lost property, and if anythink was to 'appen to 'er, why, there'd be some'ut to pay, I can tell you! That's all my little story, but I thought it would 'elp to pass the time away. Don't yer feel a bit more comfortable now, Mr. Griffith?"

"My legs—oh, my legs!" groaned the manager.

"Hold still," said Shadow, "and I'll see if I can't shift the stuff a bit."

But the rock had jammed them down too tight to move. He struggled to straighten his knees and push back the weight of coal, but then the crumbling falls began again, blocking out what little air was left. The heat was becoming unendurable.

"Give over," said the manager; "I'm dying of thirst. Can't a man even die decent in this shaft?"

"I've got a bit of cogwood for the sick pony. That'll keep us from gettin' clemmed," said Shadow, and with great difficulty he drew the bread and cheese warm from his pocket, and began putting it into the manager's mouth.

"It ain't no good," said Griffith, choking. "I'm goin', Shadow, I'm goin'. Remember me kind to my wife. Nellie her name is. I know I ain't been much of a 'usband towards 'er, but I do 'ope she'll think on me kind."

"Oh yes, you've been all right," said Shadow. "You wasn't 'alf bad."

"Couldn't yer put up a bit of a prayer, Shadow?"

"Not me," said Shadow. "I never knowed one, and I should 'ope there ain't no call for it neither. Why, you'll live to be a Butty, don't fret yerself."

Nevertheless, in the deep bass voice which

Nature had given him as a joke, he began to sing the one verse he knew:

> "'Hold the fort, for I am coming,'
> Jesus signals still;
> Wave the answer back to heaven,
> 'By Thy grace, we will.'"

The words had stuck in his head because he thought they were a war-song, and they reminded him of the breezy flags in the signallers' squad at Birmingham. But he knew no more; so he sang that verse over and over again, starting each time with renewed energy, but getting weaker and weaker towards the end. Now and then he would stop and say, "Are you alive or dead, Mr. Griffith?" and then, as no answer came, he went on singing again. And as the minutes and hours of darkness slowly crept by, he himself lost knowledge of where he was, and passed into a world of visions. It seemed to him that he was indeed Wellington in person, standing in the centre of the long low ridge at Waterloo, waiting and watching for the moment of the battle's crisis. A gentle drizzle fell. His horse shivered under him. Would the Prussians ever come? His men died as they lay. And all the time he sang "Hold the fort," and waited.

And so in the evening, after long hours of careful digging, the rescue party found him. His lips were seen to move, and as a lamp was shone in his eyes, he was heard to whisper, "Hold the fort." Both men were so tightly clasped in unconscious sleep that to save time they were sent up together just as they were in the cage.

It was sunset, and all Wenley was gathered round the pit. Within the enclosure Mrs. Griffith stood alone, and waited for her husband. The story of how the bodies were found had already spread, and at the sight of the cage a deep murmur arose from the crowd. The doctor received its burden, and tenderly disentangled the stiffened limbs. "He's alive—your husband's alive," he said, looking up with joy at Mrs. Griffith.

Then she fell on her knees, and putting her arms round Shadow's neck, she kissed him like a little child as he lay.

"Bless 'im!" sobbed all the women. "Her's got some'ut to be grateful to 'im for."

Then she turned to attend to her husband,

whose legs were crushed almost beyond hope of cure.

Before the end of the week Shadow came back to work again. As he approached the pit he wore a shamefaced air, not entirely due to the cheer which his mates raised at sight of him. Kneeling all that time down in the pit had worn great holes in his trousers. Being a shifty little man, he had patched them with new bits of corduroy; but they had lost their military beauty, and stuck out unseemly on each side. "Why, Shadow," said the huge Butty, clapping him on the back, "thee's gone quite bow-legged!"

"Please, sir, it ain't me," said Shadow, drawing himself up with modest dignity; "it's my trouseys."

Then he went down with the rest, and the ponies almost broke their halters with joy at hearing his quick footstep again.

IV

ON THE ROAD TO PARNASSUS

IT was a Saturday night in summer, and Wenley had laid itself out for the weekly delirium of enjoyment. From the level ground at the foot of the long hill, the roar of a steam merry-go-round could be heard far away by less fortunate villages, as solemn couples went whirling round upon its wooden horses to the tune of an obsolete song, tortured into a waltz. A cheap-jack rattled plates together, uttering shrill warnings of lost opportunity to the heedless. Women hastened up and down with gossip and protestations, maintaining the standard of each other's duty. Public-houses glowed with lights, and sounded with emphatic voices. After the grinding toil of the week, the moment of compensation had come. All were possessed by the frenzy for pleasure, and across the paradise of the blessed Sabbath the dreariness of Monday morning looked almost as remote as death.

A boy and a girl came out of one of the inns at the bottom of the village, and began slowly to climb the upward road, with its deep covering of loose black dust. They seemed little more than children, but in her arms she hugged their skinny child along.

"Weren't it warm in there!" he said, taking off his cap and wiping his forehead with it. His hair hung over his pale and regular face in dark-reddish locks.

"You're right," she answered. "It's a sweet mercy I sold my petticoat, or I dunno whatever I'd do for heat."

"Well, and 'ow do yer think my song went?" he asked, after a pause.

"It was an 'eavenly success, dear, and no mistake," she said. "I seed a pitman laughin'."

"What did us make?" he asked again.

"Sixpence by the petticoat," she answered.

"And what by the singin'?"

"Well," she said, "I got seven 'alfpence."

"It ain't much," he said, with a sigh.

"No," she answered, "it ain't to be called very much, but it all mounts up. And ninepence 'alfpenny's a pretty fair start for the week."

"Sixpence of it was for yer petticoat," he objected.

"And who said it weren't?" she replied. "And besides, I've got my boots to sell, and I'd a deal sooner be without 'em in this doost."

"But yer've got nothink worth the sellin' after that," he said.

"Money ain't the only thing," she retorted.

"Why, what else is there?" he asked.

"Yer've often told me, there's the glory."

"Oh yes," he answered, "there's the glory."

"To be sure," she went on, "us could do with a bit of some'ut beside, just to buy the baby a new belly-band, seein' he's fair bustin' the tapes off his'n with swellin' so fat."

"Mary," he said, stopping in the middle of the road and turning on her, "yer know very well it ain't swellin' fat no more nor us. It ain't no good makin' believe."

"You don't know nothin' about him," she said. "He's all right, and as fat as it's good for 'im to be. But oh, I do sometimes wish I'd 'ad a lot of babies before, so as to be quite sure what's right to do for this here one."

She drew aside the shawl which covered her own head and the baby too, and looked down at its pinched little face.

"I tell yer what it is," said David, walking on in front: "if us don't take a deal more at the next public, I'll do some'ut as'll rid yer of me for ever, and a good job too."

"Now, don't get talkin' that way," she said, rubbing her eyes. "I ask it of yer, don't! I can't abear it when you're took like that. You keep on smilin', and I'll cadge the money right enough."

They said no more, but tramped on till they came where the Bull's Head flared across the road and cast a dubious light on the grey church opposite. Pushing the swing-door open, they stood side by side in the midst of the public tap-room.

The place was full of smoke and noise and the smell of beer. The benches round the walls and the two wooden tables were crowded with customers—quarrymen brown from the earth, pitmen still unwashed, chain-makers with hands scarred by the forge. Women were there too—some with their husbands, taking one turn in three at the men's quarts;

some drinking in their own right as wage-earning nailers. The chubby landlord, bustling about, was pleased at the arrival of the singers, for the argumentative stage among his patrons was verging towards the quarrelsome. A few were sleepily gazing in front of them, abandoning themselves to a stupefied luxury of rest, like oxen loosed from the plough. A few were still grumbling over unjust hardships of their own. But most, inspired by that strange passion for nobler things, were striving to penetrate into regions where the torpid intellect might for a brief space find exercise. An Irishman was tracing the distress of his land to the introduction of flax, which had exhausted a soil once so rich in saints and heroes, and he was offering to settle the question for ever by fighting a "creeping Saxon" who doggedly maintained that cabbage would have been worse even than flax. The Wenley Radical was drawing a parallel between Beaconsfield and Napoleon, because both were "Crossican Jews" from Poland, in league against the working-man. Old Issachar was maintaining the advantages of education; thanks to which his grand-daughter Alice would always be able to read the murders and wife-beatings and divorces in the paper of a Sunday for herself, instead of being dependent on grandchildren for the news, as he was. "And how's I to know her don't skip the best o' the penn'orth?" he was asking appealingly; but perceiving the new arrivals in the middle of the floor, he glared at them in silence like the rest.

Clutching his cap in both hands, David at once began to sing, his eyes fixed on vacancy. Mary glanced timidly round the audience, as though to estimate the chances of favour; and then arranging the shawl so that the women might just see the baby's little white head peeping above it, she turned to David, and waited for his signal to join in the chorus. She stood under the gas-light, a pretty and girlish figure. Her wild brown hair escaped under the edge of the shawl. Her thin and shrunken skirt hung close to her limbs, and showed the bare ankles and bulging boots below.

The first song was the usual popular ballad, such as filters through the country from music-halls and suburban drawing-rooms. It bewailed the inconstancy of mortal affections contrasted with the diamonds which still flashed from false Love's finger. Without any feeling of incongruity, the audience, led by Mary's high treble, growled out the familiar words of the chorus:

> "The Duke's high window's ablaze with light,
>   There's a whisper of feet on the floor;
> She is dancing, is dancing, my love to-night,
>   My love who is mine no more."

With eyes bent on the ground, each taking care not to look at his neighbour for fear of being put to open shame for committing such an act as singing, the villagers sang it steadily through to the very last verse. Then, with a sense of a duty performed at all costs, they lifted their toil-stained faces, and with heavy feet stamped their satisfaction on the bricks and sawdust.

In answer to the applause, Mary smiled round the circle to keep them in good-humour. She was very anxious for the success of the next song. It was of David's own making, and she knew that on its reception his happiness and temper depended till the next time he sang it again. He began at once:

"As I went up and down the world,
　　I made a little song,
And sang it to the fields and woods,
　　Whilst wandering along;
Upon the breezes it was borne,
　　And carried by the birds,
The men all loved the tune of it,
　　The women loved the words."

With kindling eyes Mary led the chorus, her whole body swaying to mark the time and emphasis:

"Singing, 'No road need I to travel by,
　　No compass and no chart,
And the only star in all the sky
　　For me's my true love's heart.'"

No one joined in the words, for they were new; but the more polite grunted to keep her company. Then David went on:

"The queen she sang it on the throne,
　　Wearing her golden crown,
The sailors sang it out at sea,
　　The gentlefolk in town,
The soldiers on the battlefield,
　　The shepherds by their sheep;
And mothers put their little ones
　　At night with it to sleep.

Singing, 'No road need I to travel by,'" &c.

> "The baker he was singing it
>   From whom I stole the bread,
> The p'liceman when he collar'd me
>   Had my song in his head,
> The judge he sang it on the bench,
>   The witness in the box,
> And now I hear my gaoler's voice
>   As he turns the prison locks,

Singing, 'No road need I to travel by,'" &c.

Mary sang "For me's my true love's heart" twice over to show that was the end. Then Shadow, the "'oss-fettler," from an unobserved corner suddenly cried, "Brayvo, moother!" There was a roar of laughter; and whisking off one of her baby's socks, Mary held it out to him for alms with an open-hearted smile. Making a stiff military bow, Shadow dropped a halfpenny into it, and other coppers followed as she passed round the tables with the simple appeal. The women clucked like hens to please the baby. The men said "moother," and every time they said it the whole room laughed again.

Then she turned as usual into the bar-parlour, where the plutocracy of labour sit beside their nectar, and listen to the sounds of savage mirth from the tap-room, pleasantly subdued by distance. As she hurried across the short dark passage, she ran against the landlord, who was waiting there.

"Look 'ere," he whispered, holding her by the arm, "I've took a fancy to you. Whose child's that you've got?"

"Thank yer kindly," she said, shaking him off, "and whose should it be?"

"Now," he went on, "'ere's two shillin' for yer, and all you've got to do is to say that child ain't yourn, if the question's put to yer."

"And what's the good of talkin' like that?" she asked.

"Take the two shillin', and don't ask stoopid questions," he said. "Now mind, you've only got to say you hired it out for the look of the thing."

He forced the money into her hand. "Well," she said, spitting on it for luck, "if it's only for a say-so, there ain't no harm done."

She crept past him, hastily lifted the latch of the parlour door, and entered. "Spare a trifle for the poor little baby, mum," she said, holding out the little sock to a stout woman on the "screen." It was a Doggie's wife.

"No tramps nor no hussies for me, thank yer," she answered, swelling and ruffling like an indignant turkey. "Why can't people do work same as the rest of we has got to, instead of goin' round singin' and doin'? It's against nature. And a baby too!"

"Please, mum, he ain't against nature," said Mary, and stopped short.

"Now, my girl," broke in Mr. Johnson, the engineer, speaking as much as possible like the chairman of a vestry, "some of we has been takin' a look at yer through the tap-room hinges, and the landlord has laid an even five shillin' against the Doggie as that child ain't yer own. Now, tell the truth, yes or no. And remember, five shillin' depends on yer answer."

Mary held the two shillings tight in her left hand, and glanced anxiously round the room. She pressed the baby so close to her that it began to wake and stir against her side. "Whose else should 'e be?" she whispered, looking down.

"Never you mind for whose else, so long as it ain't yourn," put in the landlord quickly.

She made no answer.

"You see," said the landlord, looking round in triumph, "her can't say it. Now, don't be frightened, my dear. You hired it, didn't yer?"

"What should I want hirin' of 'im for, when I got 'im for nothin'?" she said.

"Oh, it was give yer!" said the landlord. "Anyways, the thing ain't yer own child."

"Who dares to say he ain't my own child?" she cried, turning savagely on the man. "I s'pose I'd ought to know best."

The room shouted applause. "Quite right," laughed the Doggie's wife, rubbing her knees. "A course her'd ought to know best. I've moothered eight, thank God, and if I do get a bit mixed up over them last five or six, I don't forget the first, no, nor shan't, not to my dyin' day. There, my dear, there's a nice penny for the baby, and I don't begrudge it, seein' he's won a fair five shillin' for my 'oosband and me. But you tell that young man it ain't right to take a girl like you slotherin' over the country at night and doin' no work."

"Please, mum, we's got our singin' to do," said Mary, with a curtsey of thanks for the penny.

"Singin'! Call *that* work?" cried the woman, and the whole room joined in her scornful laugh as Mary went out, the landlord following close behind her.

He shut the door, and seizing her round the

neck, dragged the shawl from her head, and turned her face up to his. "You vixen," he said.

"All right," she answered, beginning to cry. "Here's yer money."

"Kiss me quiet, and yer may stick to it," he whispered.

"Let me go! What do yer take me for?" she cried. But at that moment she heard David's voice beginning their last song. She thought of his threat and of the few, the very few half-pence she had collected. The silver seemed to glow in her hand. With a quick movement she drew the shawl right over the baby's head so that he could not see, and shut her eyes, holding her pale little face rigid. The moment the man's lips touched her she tore herself away, and sprang into the pitiless gas-light of the tap-room, where every eye turned curiously upon her. She was just in time to join David in the chorus:

"Hi! hi! clear the way
For the rowdy-dowdy boys!"

and as she sang, she tried with her right hand to twist up her knot of brown hair, which had somehow fallen loose.

"O David," she said, as they passed from the glaring room into the blue air of the summer night, "ain't there a 'orse-trough nowheres hereabout?"

"Do yer want to bath the baby?" said David.

"Baby, indeed! at this time of night!" she answered.

"Well," said David, "if yer want a drink, that seems a pretty big pond there."

"I only wish it was the sea," she said, and handing him the child, she knelt by the edge of the duck-pond, and plunged her face into the water. Then she rubbed her cheeks and mouth with her hands, and dried herself carefully with the bottom of her skirt.

"Well?" he said at last, in the voice of one who hardly ventures to know the worst.

"Oh, grand!" she laughed. "Guess 'ow much!"

"I counted over fivepence," he said.

"Fivepence!" she cried in scorn. "Why, three shillin' won't buy we now. What do yer say to two and sevenpence halfpenny at one go?"

"It can't be true!" he said.

"What's that, then, dear?" she asked, jingling the money in her pocket as she ran along the edge of the pond, and threw her arms round his neck. "Kiss me."

"If us could keep that up, it 'ud be a pound a week, not countin' Sundays," he said.

"Why, it's a deal better than doin' work," she answered, kissing his neck as she softly took the baby back. "Thee's great at singin', David. I always knowed it."

"Ain't it glorious!" he said. "But let's get along to Doodley, and have a nice clean bed. We might run to a sixpenny to-night, mightn't us, dear?"

And as they trudged along the upland road, with its wide views over the flaring and smoking land, all silvered by the moon, he kept repeating softly to himself the two lines of the hymn:

> "Those amaranthine bowers
> Unalienably ours."

He had no idea what the words meant, but their length and strangeness pleased his poetic sense.

"I'm thinkin'," said Mary at last, "unless your dear 'eart's set on gettin' into a bed to-night, I'd just as leave sleep out, and spend the sixpence on baby's underclothin'."

They turned aside to a deserted pit, standing lonely in the middle of its old refuse-heaps. David shook the engine-house door, but it was tight fastened. Then they found the shaft. The mouth had been boarded over some feet below the surface, and old planks and railings had fallen across the top, making a kind of roof. David cautiously lowered himself on to the platform, and struck a match. "That's first rate," said Mary, "so long as them boards don't drop us down the shaft into the water! The p'lice won't never think of lookin' for we here."

So there they made their home for the night, and had supper on the bread and sweets they had hidden in their pockets. Then she fed the baby, and spreading out the shawl over all three, she pretended to go to sleep.

"What are yer ditherin' for? Can't yer 'old still?" said David, after a while.

"I ain't ditherin', dear," she answered; "but I'm sorry I sold that petticoat now."

"What are yer cryin' for, Mary?" he asked again.

"I ain't cryin', dear," she said; "but I'd ought to 'ave knowed you'd make the money all right."

"Ain't it grand!" he said. "And there's the glory as well."

"Yes, there's the glory, a course," she answered; and he fell asleep warm and happy against her side.

V

HIS EWE LAMB

"THEY devour widows' houses." It was literally true of the pits round Wenley. They devoured every kind of house above them. Ages ago the old Earth there laid down her grand seam of the "thick coal" at no great depth from the present surface. Thirty or forty feet thick it runs, and can be scooped out like butter. Through its full height the miners drive their "workings"; and when a limit is reached, they turn and work back, cutting away, as they go, the great "pillars" or solid supports of coal, and leaving only a hollow void. Into this void the surface gradually settles down—"crowns in," as the people say—and then the houses of the poor begin their dance of death. Some bow forward; some curtsey back; some raise, as it were, one foot to heaven, whilst the other plunges into the grave. The uneasy inhabitants exclaim, "That's them pits!" and cut the legs of their beds and tables to suit the pitch of the floors, in hopes of restoring the comfort of the horizontal. Then they gird the houses round with iron rods screwed tightly together, and shaw up the bulging sides with wooden beams, and stuff the gaping cracks over the doors and windows with mortar and old stockings. If the worst befalls, they creep away disconsolate to what more stable covert they can find. The law has secured to the great lords who own the pits the right of working them on this peculiar method. Shall not a man do what he will with his own? Besides, as one of the lords genially remarked, they give employment to thousands. And, but for their ownership, it could not be supposed that sane men would ever have thought of working the pits for themselves.

One morning, therefore, a great lord's agent announced that the workings of Pit Number Nine were to be driven under Paradise Bank, and sent due notice bidding the people clear out as soon as possible, because it was thought the thick coal came very near the surface there. Paradise Bank heard and shuddered. It was not a village in its own right, but a green and pleasant oasis which had grown up at random on a long, low spur of Wenley Hill. Houses were scattered over it, a few in little red-brick rows of six or seven side by side, with sweets and dried herrings for sale in the windows. But most had been run up by the owners on little plots of garden fenced in from the old chase or waste. The smartest had been purchased with steady thrift by means of Building Societies. All their lives the poor had been told that thrift alone could save them. With flesh and blood they had practised thrift, and now they had their reward. True, they ought to have been more prudent still. When they set about building, they ought to have pursued legal inquiries, and discovered that the law would allow them no protest or compensation for their ruin. If the working-classes do not possess knowledge, forethought, self-restraint, and the other virtues, how can they expect to be happy? Happiness depends on character, as any philanthropist would gladly have told them for nothing.

So the agent published his decree, and Paradise Bank shuddered and obeyed. Every evening when work was done, some little procession might be seen wending away from the spot, seeking a neighbouring shelter from which to watch what might befall the old home. In front went the man, pushing a hired barrow on which were piled the chests of drawers, the chairs, the bedding, and other "bits of things," which had all looked decent enough in their familiar places, but now lay naked to contumely, turned upside down, and piteously exposed. Behind went the wife, dragging the children along, or wearily restraining their joyful excitement at the change. In a few weeks the place was deserted, and cats ran wild about its silent lanes. All else had gone, except, indeed, the owner of one trim little cottage in the very middle of the Bank.

Treacle Tim had himself once been a pikeman in Pit Number Nine, and had been esteemed a hard-working and sagacious collier. Three or four years before this, however, he had been "pinched a bit sharp," as he modestly put it, by a fall of "stuff," and had retired from the mine to his cottage and garden-plot, as a philosopher might. No one knew exactly what he had suffered, but it must have been something pretty bad; for it was reported that, in order to quiet any claim for compensation, the great lord sent him a regular supply of coal, with his compliments, every month. Excellent coal it was, and abundant too—all the neighbourhood knew that; for there was much more than a lonely man like Tim could use for himself, and he was able to retail large quantities at very moderate prices to nearly all the householders of Paradise Bank. "Share and share alike— that's my way of lookin' at it," he used to say, with cheerful generosity. Sometimes at night sounds of carts were heard coming up to Tim's dwelling and then lumbering heavily away. There was nothing in that to cause surprise in a land where so many work by night. "Hullo!" murmured the neighbours between their dreams. "There's Treacle's compensation coomin' oop. What a mercy it must be to have met with an accident!"

Tim had been married; his wife was a North Staffordshire girl; but about a year after he left the mine, she went visiting, and had not since been heard of. When questioned as to her fate, Tim would reply with the simple resignation of the natural man, that 'she was below the ground; and he would perhaps add some weighty observation on the general course of human life. For, like many silent countrymen, Tim had an art of pregnant sentence, and his neighbours called him a "scholard." He always spent the long mornings in strict seclusion, but in the spacious leisure of a summer afternoon it would have gladdened the heart of any idyllic poet of the poor to have seen him sitting under the shade of the Cyclopian walls which he had piled round his garden with the choicest masses of his compensation coal, and carefully protected with whitewash against the weather. In his hand, from which time seemed unable to erase the ingrained marks of labour, he would hold a book; or perhaps with sprawling pencil he would note down on a slip of paper some splendid thought, borne into his mind as he meditated to the sound of innumerable bees. From time to time he would rise, and with hoe or rake visit the garden-beds, lovingly tending his favourite plants as a shepherd tends his sheep.

For, as became a philosopher, his garden was his consolation and his pride. Bit by bit he had almost imperceptibly added to it by throwing forward his walls. Within a radius of three miles round Wenley it was spoken of with respect. Once a real lady had stopped her carriage at the gate in admiration, and Tim had offered her some sweet-william seed, with the words, "A poor man's gift is a gift twice given." His vegetables took prizes at Sedgeley Wake, one of the festivals which, like the "Whitsun feets," marked the religious year, and were supposed to keep the poor content in their labours. A leek of his, exhibited there, was already on the way to become a myth, and its reported weight had slowly risen from two pounds to three. Peas and scarlet runners grew thick as hedges over their branching sticks. There were the potatoes and lettuces and spring-onions in tidy rows. Cabbages Tim never grew, as being vulgar things. But there was something dainty and well bred about his deep-set celery-beds, carefully banked and sheltered. In the midst of the garden stood a large greenish dome of semi-transparent glass, the first appearance of which had excited much curiosity. Tim called it a "radiator," and frankly owned it was the secret of all his success. Some of the neighbours erected a similar dome in their gardens, and one or two noticed a considerable improvement in the growth of their plants; but to most it seemed to make little difference. "Nay," said Tim, "Nature don't lead them wrong as reads her right; but to read her right you wants to get at her 'eart." Close round the white cottage itself old-fashioned English flowers blossomed in profusion, and the porch was covered with roses, red and yellow. When the north or easterly wind brought over Wenley the full horror of Black Country smoke, Tim would wash the leaves at night with soapy water. Over the entrance-door he had painted up the words, "The Reward of Skill and Industry"; and certainly no one begrudged the poor man his innocent self-satisfaction.

But now that the decree of doom had gone out, many pitied him, and wondered what he would do. He did nothing. His brain seemed paralysed by the misfortune. He appeared not to understand what the notice meant. The threatened disaster was surely too appalling ever to be realised. He watched the others remove their goods and go, with unquestioning indifference. All this fuss and protestation did not seem to concern him. Passers-by saw him wandering about his garden or sitting in the fragrant shade as usual. Nay, on his face there seemed a deeper calm, an appearance perhaps of such relief as an anchorite might feel when a rival in the desert departed from a neighbouring cave. The agent, hearing of the peculiar hardship of the case, went one evening, contrary to his custom, to visit Tim in person, and addressed him with angry remonstrance.

"I tell you," he said, "I'm pretty nearly sure the coal's going to crop out under your very house. In six weeks time that garden won't be a garden nor yet a pit. It'll be an open quarry."

"You knows more nor me, a course," Tim answered. "But you can't never know what Nature'll be doin' of next, unless you love 'er same as a female."

"What's the good of talking stuff?" cried the agent.

"Well," said Tim, "maybe there's a trooble."

A "trouble" or "fault" is a sudden break or shifting in a seam—perhaps even its disappearance.

"Trouble or not," said the agent, "I tell you for the last time, if you stop, you go to perdition at your own risk."

"I'm a poor man," answered Tim, "but it would be small coomfort to me to go to perdition at yourn."

"As you like," cried the agent, turning to go. "I'm coming round to-morrow to have a look at the ground hereabouts, and I'll stake my life and reputation there's yards of coal lying only a few feet under those vegetable beds."

"Your life and reputation wouldn't be no good to me," said Tim, "or I'd take on the bet willin'. But a course it ain't to be expected for a poor man same as me to know nothin' about such things."

As the agent passed through the gate, he met a comely young woman on the point of entering. Had he been better acquainted in Wenley, he would have recognised her as Harry Barton's widow. "Good evening, Mr. Treacle," she said, going up to the porch under which the victim of the lust for riches was still standing in meditation, gazing at the sunset sky with a far-away look in his eyes. "I thought I'd drop in and see if you was perhaps enjoyin' bad health owin' to your misfortunes."

"Unless above himself he can erect himself, how vain a thing is man," Tim answered quietly. "It was only this afternoon I wrote that down with my own hand."

"It won't be a matter of erection," she said, "when you've crowned in, same as Mrs. Wilson's cow three years gone, as was never seen nor heard no more, milk and meat and all. It's ruin, Tim, or maybe worse."

"There's a many kinds of ruin," said Tim. "Some's bad, some ain't so very."

The widow looked at him quickly. She had heard strange rumours about Tim lately, and some one had seen a great heap of gold sovereigns in the bank with his name written over it.

"I'm speakin'," Tim continued, "of the ruin of 'eart and mind."

"A course," said the widow, "that kind of ruin don't seem to make much odds, do it?

Not so long as the money's safe. But I'd like to speak a word to you on that very thing, if you'd let me coom in."

"Speak it out 'ere," said Tim. "The inside's 'ardly fit for no lady now." And he sighed, as though mindful of his loss.

But she gently edged past him into the living-room, and sat down. It was growing dark, but she looked curiously round at the old polished furniture, the china, the solemn clock, and other signs of prosperity.

"What a wonder of a man you are, Tim!" she said, "everything's almost as neat and nice as if I'd kep' it myself. I s'pose a man like you don't hardly feel the want of a woman's hand about the place?"

"No," said Tim, "I can't say as I do—not pertikler."

"But isn't it lonesome of an evenin'?" she asked. "Don't you ever miss her as was?"

"No," said Tim; "there's always my own contented heart for coompany."

"There's some feels lonesome," said the widow, with a little sigh. "But you do seem to live very nice."

"I've no cause to complain," said Tim.

"Agricoolture do pay, so long as a man keeps 'isself poor."

"Poor and single, I s'pose," she said with a little glance up at him. "But there's some gives out you're not so poor after all."

"Ay," said Tim, "and I'm afeard they'll be sayin' next I'm not single neither."

"O Tim, how you talk!" said the widow, getting up as if to go, but laying her hand beside his on the table. "Now, all I've got to say is to entreat of you to leave this house afore it crowns in with you and all. I'll give up my place to you, and welcome, and I'll stop with my sister. There's plenty of room in my little house, and nice and quiet too, now poor Harry's gone."

"Thank you kindly," said Tim, "and I'll bear in mind to ask the favour of you some day. But there ain't no pertikler hurry at this present."

"O Tim, you're a poor lone man as me a woman," she said; "be careful of yourself for my sake."

She had taken his hand as though to say good-night, but did not let it go.

At that moment footsteps were faintly heard,

as of some one coming up stone stairs with a heavy load, and a cry of "Lilycock, lilycock!"—the old call of the North Staffordshire miners at the change of shifts—seemed to rise from the depths of the earth. Then an orange light flickered and danced through the darkening room. It flashed between the chinks of the coal-cellar door under the bedroom stairs. With a crash the door itself was flung wide open. In a blaze of light a woman's form stood revealed. It was very sparely clad. The skin and clothing were blackened and begrimed. The face shone like burnished metal. In one hand flared a smoking candle. The other clutched a dark and weighty sack slung over the shoulder.

"Time's oop, Tim," said a deep voice. "Didn't yer hear me callin' to you to coom below?"

That face, that voice—where had the widow known them before? Without so much as a scream, she turned and fled through the garden.

"A bad conscience," said Tim reflectively, "is a disturbin' thing to keep coompany with—more especial if it's a female."

"Didn't know you was keepin' coompany, or I wouldn't have coom oop," said the form.

"Maria," said Tim, "our game's pretty nigh played out. We'll 'ave to do what's called surrender at discretion."

"Never whiles I live!" cried the form, swinging the heavy sack to the ground with a gasp of exhaustion.

"Well," said Tim, "we'll spring a mine on 'em fust anyways." So saying, he put on strange and blackened apparel, and taking the light in his hand, he disappeared in his turn behind the cellar door.

Next day about noon the agent returned, as he had threatened, and found Tim meditating as usual by the garden wall. In his hand he held a loose coil of rope. Without taking any notice of him, the agent walked up and down the beds, turning up the soil here and there with the point of his stick.

"This ain't the best time of year for hoeing," Tim remarked.

"What's that thing for?" asked the agent, pointing to the glass dome.

"That's called a radiator," said Tim, with the air of a National School teacher. "It gathers up the rays of the sun, and spreads 'em about through the earth's vitals."

"How's that managed?"

"By reason of a deep hole," said Tim. "I've read in my books as Nature's an open secret. Well, that's my way of getting at that there secret. You can look for yourself."

With effort he lifted the glass dome away, and revealed a large dark hole, lined with bricks round the top.

The agent lay flat on the ground and peered into it. "Why," he said, "that's the very thing I want for examining the seam. I'll squeeze down it."

"Not you," said Tim. "It's twelve yards deep or more, I warn yer."

"What's that rope for? Wouldn't it bear me?"

"Well," said Tim, "I mostly uses it for tyin' oop my carnations. But maybe it 'ud do for tyin' you oop just as well."

So he fastened it tight under the agent's arms, and fastened the other end round a large apple-tree. Then the agent slowly descended, supporting himself with his back and knees, whilst the rope was paid out bit by bit. As he went down he kept striking matches and examining the sides.

"I told you so," he called out at last.

"Told me what?" said Tim.

"Why, the thick coal crops out right at the surface of your garden."

"What crops out?" shouted Tim.

"Why, the coal—the thick coal."

"Crops out where?" cried Tim, unfastening the rope from the apple-tree.

"Why, here, in your garden," said the agent.

"Oh, I knowed that," said Tim, in a disappointed tone, and let the rope drop down the hole on the agent's head.

Then stooping down, he shouted: "Maria! Maria! just take the light with thee, and coom oop the down-cast shaft, and mind ye lock the two doors at top. His lordship's bringin' out a patent for radiators, and the agent wants to see ourn at work and lightin' oop our mine."

Then he replaced the heavy glass dome over his "up-cast shaft," and taking his seat on the top of it, lit his pipe with leisurely care.

It was never known on what terms the agent was released. But he was obliged to confess to himself that he had never seen a mine better laid out than Treacle Tim's. A "fort," or mass of solid coal and rock, had been left under the cottage itself, except where a neat staircase of nearly fifty steps led down from the cellar to a miniature "sump." The galleries had been worked on a system of "pillars," so that the surface was undisturbed. In fact it was a fairy palace of a mine. When asked afterwards why he countermanded his order to carry Pit Number Nine in that direction, the agent used to say it would not have paid his lordship, owing to a peculiar trouble or interruption in the seam. "Besides," he would add, "there were other reasons."

In the evening many neighbours naturally collected round the cottage to learn the truth about Widow Barton's adventure. They found Tim standing on a chair under the porch, and painting out the words "The Reward of Skill and Industry."

"Yes," he said surlily, "there's talk of stoppin' my compensation."

"And what are you goin' to call the cottage now?" they asked.

"Naboth's Vineyard," he answered.

"Maria!" he then called out, "as you ain't workin' day-shift just now, hand us up some more paint."

Then the late Mrs. Treacle Tim came from the cottage, and meekly held the paint-pot.

VI

AN ANTI-SOCIAL OFFENDER

IT was getting late one Sunday night in October, but the Wenley doctor and his guest were still sitting over the study fire and talking upon problems of modern life, with the heightened enthusiasm of middle age. The doctor's old friend Professor Parker had come down from London to stay with him for a few days, and had that evening delivered a lecture, illustrated by lantern slides, upon "The Duties of the Citizen," in the little hall where the doctor tried to assemble a few working-people in hopes of inspiring them with some slight interest in "the things of the mind."

"The people here," the professor was saying, "are scattered over the land like sheep with the rot. Unorganised, disunited, they are helpless in the hands of the capitalist. The local industries are slowly dying out. Yet the people increase without pause. I never saw so sad a sight as that school play-ground, crammed with happy children shouting at their play. They are the hopeless toilers of the future. Why do they exist? I could never understand what the economic reason for marriage among working-people precisely is."

"It is hard indeed to discover it," said the doctor.

"Their never-ending reproduction is distinctly anti-social," continued his friend. "Where would the power of capitalist and landowner be if it stopped? A universal strike could not be so effectual, and would be far more difficult to organise."

"The proposal sounds delightfully simple, certainly. If only reason ruled the world!"

"Well," said the professor vehemently, "I can see no real hope for the future as long as the working-classes continue to offer their children to the Moloch of industrial slavery. They must thwart the employers by refusing to breed slaves for them. That is what I shall preach."

"Preach away!" said the doctor, with a sigh. "I wish you success with all my heart. But it must be nearly two o'clock, and I shall have to get some sleep, pleasant as it is to have some one to talk to as in the good old days."

As they went into the passage, there was a violent alarum at the door. The night-bell rang, the telephone at the doctor's bedside whistled like a far-off engine. Loud cries of "Doctor" and "Perlice" came from the porch.

"I only wish you'd begun your preaching earlier," said the doctor wearily. "There's some poor woman never heard of it. On these occasions the husband always shouts 'Police!' because he thinks nothing else would get me out of bed. Well," he continued, opening the door, "which of you is it?"

But it was the police in person.

"Beg pardon, sir. Peculiar case. Two prisoners in the new white-tiled cell. One female; the other infant, sex unknown, apparently child of female. Found them in the main street at 12.30 A.M., both howling, female trying to run. Took them in charge for drunk and disorderly without visible means. Female said she must run to Stafford. Told her she couldn't. Her threatened to hang 'erself.

AN ANTI-SOCIAL OFFENDER 97

Told her she mustn't take the law into her own hands. Violently assaulted me; might have done me bodily harm; but wouldn't let go on the infant. Put them comfortable in best cell, and went to bed. Got no sleep for female shrieking and banging her body against door. Wife went and peeped in at her through slide. Said her weren't drunk, only queer in the head, and bad for infant. Asked why I didn't fetch doctor instead of laying there like a swine—begging your pardon, sir. Wouldn't give me no peace till I come. Apologise for the liberty. Peculiar case."

"All right," said the doctor; "let's go. Good-night, Parker." And he went down the wet and silent street to the cottage police-station.

The female prisoner was certainly making a terrible disturbance. He heard her cries far down the road. As he entered the cell, she dashed past him into the passage, but was held and driven back by the policeman. Clutching an almost invisible baby in her arms, she stood in the middle of the cell and glared at them both through a tangle of wet yellow hair. Though she only wore a shawl over her head, the doctor saw at once that she had put

G

on her "Sunday best," and the baby's too. But her skirt was splashed and heavy with mud. Her face was red and swollen; it seemed to blaze with delirium; and her lips were never still. He thought he had never seen so fine a representation of mere animal rage.

"Well, my good girl," he said soothingly, "what's the matter?"

"You let me out," she screamed. "I've got to run to Stafford."

"But, my dear, you couldn't run that distance to-night. You keep quiet, and we'll see about a train in the morning."

"Yes," she cried, with greater passion, "and at eight of the mornin' they'll let him out into the streets like a newly-born, and me not there to mind him! It was me as got him put in. Over seven month they've kep' him, and I ain't a-goin' to lose him now. So you just let me out."

"There, there!" said the doctor. "He'll come back to you all right. He's your husband, I suppose?"

"He's Reuben the anchor-smith, that's what he is. Everybody worth callin' knows Red

AN ANTI-SOCIAL OFFENDER   99

Reuben. And he's the father of this child, but he don't know that hisself. I've been keepin' it back from him for the purpose, me thinking it would be a pleasant surprise against his coming out."

Reflecting on the happy solicitude of her plans now frustrated, she sank upon a wooden bench and began to whimper.

"And I lost the last train," she sobbed, "only through tryin' to make the baby look respectable, and tittyvatin' it up. I couldn't abear for him to come out and set eyes on an ugly-lookin', draggle-tailed, pieced-together sort of a thing. And now he'll come out and never set eyes on nothing at all, but go straight off to her as I knows on, 'cos she's got three, and me none, so far as he reckons. And he always did have a tender 'eart, did Reuben."

"Hoosband of prisoner undergoin' sentence in Stafford County Gaol," said the policeman. "Will be released in due course this morning at eight o'clock A.M. Prisoner apprehends desertion. Beg pardon, sir, for callin' it a peculiar case."

But the prisoner had sprung up again, crying out with renewed excitement. She laid her right hand on the doctor's heart, and looked up into his face with a dog's appealing eyes.

The doctor was at a loss. He could not endure the sight of a woman's tears. He said it was because they spoilt her beauty. But he did not even affect to believe that his heart was stone to the touch of a woman's hand. As was his way, he ruffled up his grizzled hair, and for a moment he thought of the hard-working morrow and of the sleep which all men need.

"I'll get the trap out and drive her. I suppose it isn't over twenty miles. You see, constable," he added apologetically, "in these cases of acute nervous excitement it is often best to humour the patient's whims. Come, my dear, cover up the baby and we'll go."

The girl quietly obeyed. "I might have knowed as you and God would 'elp me," she said, and followed him in silence up the street to his house. When the angel delivered St. Peter from prison by night, he must have felt like her.

"Sit down and have some tea while I'm putting the horse to," said the doctor, stirring up the embers in the study, and fetching the kettle and some china.

"Thank you kindly, sir," she answered. "I don't mind if I do. And might I make so free as to ask for the use of a comb?"

Holding the hairpins between her teeth, she combed out and plaited up her long yellow hair in front of a glazed photograph of Leonardo's Virgin of the Rocks, which, being a dark picture, made in her opinion a pretty fair substitute for a looking-glass. Then she gently smoothed the sleeping baby's little fluff of reddish gold, and carefully plastered it down in front with a wetted finger, so that a fringe might show beneath the white frilling of the hood. As the doctor made the tea, he looked at her and wondered. She was now an ordinary young working-woman, practical and self-contained, displaying only an entire trustfulness in the doctor's goodwill and power. Where was the passionate feminine creature of half-an-hour ago? "In modern democracy, as in ancient hierarchy, there are things visible and things invisible," he observed to Black Auster in the stable, whilst he forced the bit into its sleepy mouth, and the loose under-lip wagged in gentle protest against harness fixed by the lantern's light.

He had soon settled the girl comfortably down in the deep corner of the trap, well under the hood, and muffled her up in rugs. She kept the baby on her lap, and as he caught sight of her face by the reflection of the carriage lamps he saw it was transfigured with joyful expectation. An undefined sense of loneliness and envy passed over his mind. No one ever looked like that in the hope of seeing *him*.

"All right now?" he asked.

"Quick, oh, be quick!" she answered, without even looking at him.

"Gratitude," he reflected to himself, "is the most meagre of all virtues, except thrift, and fortunately it can hardly be said to exist."

He called to the horse, took one glance up at the north star fitfully peering through a drift of rainy clouds, and settled down for the long drive.

"You had better lie back and go to sleep," he said, as Auster deliberately crawled up the steep slope to the top of the ridge, and he felt her stirring restlessly with impatience.

AN ANTI-SOCIAL OFFENDER

"Not me," she answered. "I'll sleep sweet enough to-morrer night, please God."

"Well," said the doctor, "you must talk then, or the horse will fall asleep. How was it Reuben got into trouble? Oh, you needn't mind telling me. I'm a doctor. I don't judge people."

They were at the top of the hill, and Auster as usual paused to rest. For miles around them the country glimmered with fire. Lucigen lights cast a white glare on cloudy pillars of smoke. Hazy fumes rose from the great blast-furnaces, unextinguished for a generation of men's lives. Orange and violet flames shot like flickering tongues of serpents from the lifted dampers of the ironworks. Sparkling eyes of crimson glowed far out among the wasted fields where ancient refuse-heaps were burning still. Near at hand the lights showed double, reflected on black canals. And over all were heard the snort and sighing of the engines, as when primeval shapes took their uneasy rest in the slime of the valleys. It seemed a cruel land, meet nurse for a savage and cruel race.

"How was it Reuben got into trouble?"

said the doctor again, looking mournfully around.

"Please, sir," said the girl, "it was all along of his havin' such a tender 'eart."

Black Auster jogged on. The doctor took one more look at the Cities of Mulciber, as he called them, and then waited, just as he always waited when a patient began by saying that he never drank.

"It was all me as done it," the girl continued. "He got summonsed for bashin' of me up."

The doctor drew in his breath, as when the patient admitted that he did take a drop now and then, at funerals, or on Saturday nights, or when he was thirsty.

"All I aimed at," she went on, "was to touch his heart, and keep him safe beside of me. But they took him away, and they've kep' him safe a deal longer than need was, through their calling it an aggravatin' assault. But it wasn't a bit aggravatin', seeing I did it for the purpose, because he has such a tender heart, has Reuben."

The doctor felt he was again losing the clue to the diagnosis of the case.

"I knew all the time," she continued, "it

came about through his having a kind of fancy for children, like what most men feel for horses and pigeons. He fair loved pawin' children about, same as a big dog with its puppies. I've often told him he was worse than any female. Not that Reuben's a female to look at, mind you."

She turned to the doctor with a smile which again brought a pang of desolate envy.

"I call to mind when first I used to see him, me going down into Cradley on arrands for my missus. I've stood more than an hour outside the shed, staring down through the window bars to see them make the anchors. One gang would be working at the shanks, and another at the crowns and flukes. But Reuben was gaffer over them that welded the crowns and shanks together, and his great red beard shone in the fire first-rate. Two of them would take the shank, and he'd nick a great bit out of the red-hot end, and jam the red-hot crown into the niche, and they'd start hammerin' at it all together. Then they'd stick the whole thing into the furnace-blast again till it looked like the sun, and pull it out, and start hammering at it again as if they could never expect to give it enough for itself. And Reuben kep' turning it round about and over, till the red began to look thick and dullish, and stop throwing off sparks. Then he'd take some water and pour on, and the water ran hissing up and down in little drops, and turned red and melted away. But each time he stopped to pour on he'd be sure to give a look up at me through the iron bars and say, 'Hullo, ducky dear! so there you are, are you?' And his mates would all start laughing, and then I'd go on for my arrands. So when winter was coming we used to meet by accident on the field-path going to Halesowen. And he wasn't long afore he took me to his home. That's two year ago last Netherton Wake."

Her voice kept up a sweet and sad melody to the steady beat of the hoofs on the wet October road. They were now passing through the very heart of the fiery and smoking land. Here and there a group of workmen, released from an early night-shift, stood revealed for a moment by the carriage lamps, were heard to speak to each other, and vanished into darkness like symbols of the generations of man.

"Two years or so isn't long to be married," said the doctor cheerily.

"Maybe not," she answered; "but one's long enough to be unhappy in."

"Why, what was the matter?"

"How old should you say my baby is?" she asked. "Well, he's four weeks next Wednesday at six in the morning, and he's the first I ever bore. That's what the matter was."

"Oh, that was it," said the doctor, and he drew the rugs more closely round her.

"Ay," she said. "It started because it got about that the girl he'd kep' company with before had laid her curse on me. And small blame to her neither, I can say now, for Reuben's a man to fill a woman's heart up. Then it so happened that the wife living next door to us had two children of her own. So every evening when Reuben was coming home, her used to take and set one child on her doorstep so as to spite me, and stand there holding the other in her arms just in time to say, 'Good evenin' to you, Mr. Reuben.' Then he'd come into our room, and find everything set nice and warm and tidy, and me ready to change his clothes like a big baby's, and only willing to do just whatever he wanted. But it all counted for no more than nothing with him, through me standing there like a thing against nature.

"So bit by bit he came to hang about next door, and stop there making a fool of himself with the children, all through his heart being so tender towards them. Next thing, her went and had a third one born, and there was I sitting in my own house, listening for its first cry. And I heard it. And so many as three times a day I counted Reuben stop and ask how that woman was getting along, for nearly the whole of that week on end. And one evening he takes and brings me in her other two brats so as to leave the house quiet for her, and sets them down to tea with us, and rolls them about on the floor, making as if he was a bear, and me sitting there neither eating nor speaking, but fit to die.

"Soon after that the woman's husband took and got killed in the mine through stuff falling on him. So Reuben goes to the burying, and comes back to the supper with the widow. And mostly every night, instead of drinking quiet in the public-house—a thing I never begrudged him—he turns in next door to cheer up that widow by talking about her insurance money. And I wasn't going to stop him, not me. I wouldn't demean myself. But there I was, sitting alone, and hearing their voices through the wall. And some people said her wasn't bad-looking, not so very."

Auster was going down hill as fast as he dared in the obscurity. The lamps of another town twinkled in front. The girl leant forward and stared with longing into the distance. Drizzling rain fell on her hot face, and covered the shawl over her head with sparkling beads.

"I suppose," said the doctor, "this little creature of yours soon put it all right."

"Oh, but it does seem a blessed long time ago," she went on. "It was bitter cold for me then, looking out of the door and waiting. And when Reuben came in, I'd say nothing, but give him something to drink and cherish him warm. And next night when he went off again I'd say nothing, through not wishing to demean myself over against that woman. So it went on till the snow started to melt, and one morning I woke and heard the water running free down the gutters into the water-tub, and the sparrows just beginning to tweet, and when I opened the door there was a kind of warm smell coming up out of the ground, and a feeling in the air as if something was going to happen. On a sudden it comes over me what that something might be; but I dursn't so much as think on it. Only day after day, deep down inside of me, as if in the bottermost pit of my heart, a kind of hope kep' on hiding itself away and then looking out again. And each day it kep' on growing, till at the last I knew for sure. And then I could never believe it.

"So one night I made everything nice as usual for Reuben, and on the horse in front of the fire I put to air a few bits of things I'd stitched ever so long before, me thinking that wouldn't be an unbecoming way of letting him know. But when he comes in I see he was more than usual contrairy, and he set straight down to his food.

"'Don't you want the hot water to wash you?' I says.

"But he just swallows down and stands up without a word.

"'Where are you going to?' I says.

"'Out,' says he.

"'Then you shan't go there never again,' I says, and I jump up and stretch my arms wide out across the door. And he stood close in front of me, three times my size, and red as guinea gold in the firelight—grand!

"'Why not?' says he, trying hard not to burst out, but I could see his veins swelling most terrible.

"'Because you shan't never go there no more again now,' says I.

"'Who's to stop me?' he says, and laughs.

"'My body, living or dead,' says I.

"'Your body ain't worth calling,' he says, and takes me round the middle and swings me away very gentle, so as to set me down by the fire. You see, he was only seeking to act kind to them poor children left alone and unpurtected. But, oh, sir, he'd never laid a hand on me before, except for loving, and it drove me wild to feel it. So what must I do but fall flat down and bash my head as hard as ever I durst upon the edge of the fender. It gashed it open fine, under the hair here, so as the blood ran down over my face and neck. But when I looked up to see how he was taking it, he was gone, and I could hear him raging about in next door and knocking down the chairs.

"So I laid down again, clutching at my heart to hold it in, and I shrieked out, 'Perlice! He's been murdering of me!' That's what I said—asking pardon of Them above for its being a lie. But I thought if only he heard me crying out he'd be sure to come back, through remembering how loving he used to be to me in the bygone. But it so happened a stupid woman of a neighbour was passing and hears me scream out, and runs for the perlice as if I was meanin' it. And then they come back together and find me laying with the blood smeared over me, and a bit of my hair burnt for the purpose in the fire, so as to go to Reuben's heart.

Then the perliceman took and fetched Reuben out and locked him up. And next morning he was had before the magistrate, and I went and swore on my solemn oath it was all a mistake, and he'd never touched me at all, but was always good and loving so far as might be. But nobody listened to the truth I was speaking, because the perlice and all the rest of them kep' on swearing to this and that, so as what with one thing and another messing about, and them calling it an aggravating assault, they went and shut him up, and have kep' him nigh on seven months from start to finish, and Them above don't know all that I've suffered along of it."

"But, my dear girl," said the doctor, looking down on her, "why on earth didn't you tell him the truth about yourself at once, and save all this trouble?"

"I dunno, sir, why it was I didn't," she said composedly, unfastening her dress and hushing the whimpering child. "I'm sure I couldn't rightly say."

"It seems to me that would have been a very easy way out of the difficulty," he went on, with a smile.

"Very easy indeed," she flashed out, "to take a poor innocent man off his guard just where you knowed the soft place in his heart! And where's the credit then for winnin' of him back? And to have that widow going around and giving out it wasn't me but the baby as had done it, and if it hadn't been for the baby comin' her could have kep' him all to herself, and me left sitting alone out in the cold! Thank you kindly, no."

"I should think not, indeed," said the doctor, wondering at masculine stupidity.

"He'll love me proper now," she murmured, "now as he'll know I'm all right, and nobody can't be sayin' nasty things. And there he is a-laying in his cell, and him not so much as dreaming that baby's born or thought on. Why, if he was to find it set out on the ground at his very feet, he'd take it up maybe and play with it, being so given to young things; but he'd never so much as suspicion it was his own, unless it might be through the colour of its hair. There ain't no telling. Me, I'd know it anywheres, though I hadn't never seen it afore; but then it's my own flesh."

"Why haven't you written to cheer him up with the news?"

"Would you have me miss givin' him the surprise when he comes out at the gate? Not likely, I should hope. And now the day's come at last. The gaoler wrote as he was goin' to open the door for Reuben on Monday at eight, and I started to run, and now I'm runnin' quicker and quicker, and there's a sound of bells—and a sound of 'armoniums playing —and a sound of Reuben calling."

The doctor felt her head fall softly against his side. He covered her from the cold morning air, and put his arm round her neck to keep her from falling. As he looked down upon her glowing but worn little face, he tried in his reflective way to unravel the twisted skein of old-fashioned emotions which had brought her there.

It was daylight now. They were in a land of plough and pasture, divided into irregular fields by hedgerows and common trees. A thick steam rose from Black Auster's back as with hanging head and labouring breath he plodded on. Steam rose from the palings and from the cows which rubbed their long throats upon the topmost bars of the gates and lowed impatiently for their keepers. All around them hung a sweet smell of milk.

"Nature is still at her old, old games," said the doctor, and drawing the girl's sleeping head closer against his side, he strove once or twice to grasp the reins more firmly, and then quietly went to sleep himself.

He was awakened by the rattle of the wheels

on paving-stones, and the merriment of some factory hands who were making emphatic comments on the situation.

"Here we are," he said, and turned aside to the gaol. A small crowd was hanging furtively about the open space in front of it, as if half afraid of being seen there. Eight o'clock struck, and suddenly a black flag appeared on one of the towers, shuddering in the cold. The crowd cheered feebly and turned white.

"Oh, mercy!" cried the girl, drawing in her breath and clutching the baby to her heart, "just think if that had been for Reuben!"

"It is for somebody," thought the doctor.

"They'll be letting him out quick now," she said.

The little portal in the prison gate opened, and a ridiculous figure emerged—a besotted, middle-aged woman, with bits of skirt flapping round her ankles. Fumbling in her pocket at the half-crown which the State had given her for a new start in life, she tottered towards the nearest group of spectators, and then turned away in another direction.

Again the portal opened, and the large figure of a working-man in corduroys stood looking

AN ANTI-SOCIAL OFFENDER

out for a moment uncertain. Then with clenched fists and eyes fixed on the ground he walked straight down the prison path.

"That's mine!" cried the girl, and laying the baby lightly in the doctor's arms, she sprang from the trap, ran through the people, and flung her arms round the man's neck. The crowd cheered and laughed with delight.

"Get off with you!" growled the man, shaking her violently away. "It's you, is it? And it was you as brought me to this—*me!*"

"Oh, Reuben dear," she said, clinging to his arm to save herself from falling. "Do what you like at me, only I've got something for you. Just come and see."

"Don't want nothing," he said, with an oath. "I've eat my breakfast already."

"It ain't exackly something to eat I've got, neither," she said, guiding him in spite of himself towards the doctor's trap. "But what do you think of that?" she cried, holding out the child.

"Dunno," said he. "What is it?"

"Well, it's called a baby," she said, laughing with joy, as she uncovered a very pink little face.

"And where did you pick that up?" he said indifferently.

"That's tellin'," she answered.

"Don't matter," he said, with a bitter laugh. "It bain't none of yourn, anyhow."

"Not properly speakin'," she answered, "'cos he's both of ourn."

He shook his head, and was turning sulkily away.

"You just look at his hair, then," she cried.

"Bless me!" he said, speaking very slowly, "look at its red 'air. Well, I *am*——and of all the——"

He put out a huge, rough finger distorted with toil, rubbed it on his trousers, and gently stroked the red feather of down which showed beneath the cap's frilling.

"Well, you *are*——" he said. "Why didn't you tell me nothing about it, you wench?"

"I thought," she said, "as maybe you'd fancy a bit of a surprise on comin' back to me."

Without another word they walked away together like people in a dream, the man carrying the child, and the woman clinging to his arm and looking up into his face.

AN ANTI-SOCIAL OFFENDER

"Poor old Parker!" said the doctor, as he led Black Auster to the stable at the inn. "Poor old Professor Parker, with his easy solution of economic difficulties by the refusal of the working classes to continue the race! I seem to hear the voice of one crying in a wilderness of babies."

VII

THE OLD ADAM

"I DO seem to 'ave made a bad job over this second, poor thing," said Abram's dying wife. "But the first was all right. Nobody can't gainsay that. He's a grand turn-out, is little Benjie, and I leave 'im to you on trust."

Her husband sat by the bedside in his Sunday coat, to show his respect for death. He spread out his great brown hands on his knees, but said nothing.

"Please God, he'll have a fine set of limbs on 'im," she continued. "Yes, he'll have that, anyways, same as yourself, Abram."

"This ain't the time to put me in mind of such things," he answered, trying in vain to speak sternly with a shaking voice.

"I wasn't born misshapen neither," she said; "so fine limbs runs in his blood, and there's no unmakin' 'im now, thank God. Let me take another look at 'im."

The man lifted up the heavy two-year child, by the back of its frock, as when one lifts a puppy by the loose skin of the neck, and all its four legs hang helplessly out.

"There's limbs," said the woman. "He'll grow to be the livin' image of what you was, Abram."

"Don't thee be speakin' on it," groaned the man. "It ain't fit to keep chewin' over such vanities so close agen the Throne."

"It's true no less," she said, putting out a feeble hand to hold the little feet which kicked against her breast. "And people'll turn to stare after 'im, same as we'd used to stare after you. And when you see 'em doin' of it, you can say, 'It was Susie Bowler growed me that son, and there ain't a woman livin' could 'ave growed 'im better.' Yes, you can say that, no matter for 'ow many you may 'ave married since me."

But Abram did not marry again. He went on living alone with his little son, and looked to the kindly offices of neighbouring mothers to do the needful mending and washing and beating for the child; and there was not a girl or woman in the place but was willing to do all that and more for the asking. They felt a kind of respect for Abram; perhaps because he never thought of paying the smallest attention to any of them.

It was a land where even the sweets for children are wrought in the shape of chains; and all the week Abram laboured at a chainmaker's forge in his own backyard. On Sundays he sat steadily through the three services in the chapel, including the infants' class. Once a year, or in exceptional seasons twice, he would stand up, his large brown face illumined by the cheerfulness of some inward light, and with extreme difficulty would speak a few unfinished sentences on the things of the soul. In all humility he envied those whose spiritual experience was rich enough to enable them to display it before the world two or three times a week. With himself, he was obliged to confess, it was otherwise. "My sperrit," he used to say, "do seem to need a deal of fettlin' oop afore it's hot."

Towards his son he scrupulously fulfilled the recognised duties of a father. He strove to keep him rigidly attentive at sermon time, and he paid a woman to cut down his own old corduroys till they might almost be said to fit the boy. In the natural course of life and the Board school, Benjie learnt various things like other children; but when he reached thirteen his education was regarded as complete, and his father was spared the rich man's anxiety of choosing which of the public schools to send him to. For, as is well known, a life of work requires just ten years less education than a life of pleasure. Accordingly, Benjie was set to work in the shed, and his father only wished the law would have allowed it two years earlier; for it is hardly possible to get along at chain-making unless one can cut down expenses by using one's own flesh and blood.

So every morning Benjie clambered up into the deep shadow of the rafters, and clinging with both hands to two chains hanging from the roof, set one foot on a little wooden platform, and with the other worked the treadle for the great bellows of the forge; for the heavy "dollied chains" which Abram made needed a greater blast than the hand-bellows of the common chain-makers could give. Platform and treadle were worn into convenient lumps and hollows by the feet of Benjie's predecessors for years past, and all day long the wind roared through the crackling gleeds, and link by link the massy chains grew longer. One afternoon a benevolent journalist, on the look-out for abuses, asked Benjie how long he could go on at the work. "Half-an-hour," came the instant reply.

"And what do you do then?"

"Take t'other foot."

"But how many hours could you work altogether?"

"Dunno."

"Don't you find the labour very distressing?"

A gleam of white teeth was visible in the obscurity of the roof as Benjie smiled in perplexity over such a problem.

"Dunno," he said, as the most satisfactory answer.

"And what do you do after work?"

"Football," shouted Benjie, hanging down from his chains, to overcome the noise of the oliver, or foot-hammer, with which his father welded the links. And the stranger closed his note-book, and turned away disappointed, for the case seemed to promise neither "copy" nor a party cry.

Football was indeed the great and sufficient joy of Benjie's heart. It had won him reputation at the Board school. For streets around, his name was spoken with reverence by every boy that breathed, and a kick from Benjie was an honour in itself. All through the long summer evenings he compelled his acquaintance to practise at the game. They played with anything that would roll—an old pair of socks carefully tied round with string, for choice. The thought that the treadle must in some way add strength to his legs, kept him steady at work through each weary hour; and every night when he went to bed he would pinch and pummel himself all over, to see if he was getting harder. Yes, he was hard, no doubt of that—"hard as nails," said the women who had helped to bring him up; "and a deal harder than them machine-made," they would add, if they were nailers themselves. "You don't make the likes of him by the gross."

When October came with the first sting of frost in the morning air, Benjie knew it was time to organise his forces. With the solemnity of a general he picked his eleven, drilled them till their "combination" was perfect, called them the Corinthians, and issued a challenge by word of mouth to any eleven of Netherton to contend for supremacy on the battlefield of the Cop, a patch of waste ground just behind Abram's shed.

It came, the long-expected day. At dawn he ran to the window. The weather was still, cold, and hazy—just perfect for the game.

"You're right to be early," said his father, getting up too. "That big cable's got to be finished to-day somehow, and it'll take we all the time till past dark."

"But it's Saturday," said Benjie.

"No matter for that. Our bit of clean must stand over till Monday."

"But it's the Corinthians!"

"What's that about Corinthians?"

"Oh, they don't matter," said Benjie, with a boy's reserve.

"No, they don't matter," said his father; "they was divided and carnal."

With a bitter heart Benjie kindled up the furnace, boiled the tea, and climbed to his post in the roof. "Then us'll get a doin'," said the Corinthian to whom he ran to tell the disastrous news at dinner-hour. The work went on again. Through a hole kept for ventilation in the roof Benjie could see most of the field. The players began to arrive. The Netherton boys brought a real football. The bladder was burst; it was stuffed with very various substances; but it was a real football. Some spectators gathered and laid imaginative wagers. The Corinthians argued and hesitated at their posts, lacking their leader's control. The umpire gave a cat-call, and with a dead thud of the ball the game began.

Like Homeric heroes, the backs at first usurped the contest, whilst the ignoble host trampled backwards and forwards in the middle and admired their chieftains. But a Corinthian back missed his kick, and an Allcomer drew close to the goal. Benjie held his breath.

"Played, Dick!" he shouted suddenly through the tiles. "Down the side with it! Now pass! Hands there! What's the good of an umpire? Now centre! Shoot, you beggar, shoot! Into him, there! Stop him down the side! Their throw! Hustle 'im in the centre!

Off side, you clummery beast! Where's that umpire? Don't let him shoot! Oh, what's the good of you all?"

A cheer went up from the Allcomers. Benjie groaned, and dropped a beat of the treadle.

"What's coom to thee?" said Abram, looking up from a meditation on the peace of God, in the midst of the blows of the oliver. "What's that hollerballoo?"

"Nothink; only a goal," said Benjie.

"Don't get backslidin' again," said his father, and the work went on. Benjie hardly cared to look from his window. All went badly for Corinth. In a few minutes another cry of pitiless triumph arose.

"Is it football they're after?" said Abram, pausing to wipe the sweat from his face. "Did you ever take a try at playin' that?"

A father never knows anything about his son.

"Yes, sometimes," said Benjie. "I'm captain of this lot."

"You captain!" cried Abram, and he smiled as he thrust the rod into the heart of the furnace and scraped the gleeds over it. "I'd used to be a bit given to diversion myself at one time. But it's a fond kind of thing. It ain't by diversion as you'll fire the devil's nest."

A third howl of joy and derision arose from the Allcomers.

"Steady with the bellows, lad, or thee'll make the iron run," said Abram. "If I was to let you off an hour or so now whiles I mend the hollybit," he went on, "could you go on treadling till Sunday strikes?"

Without a word in answer, it seemed as though a ray of light fell from the rafters and vanished through the door. It flashed out upon the field. A yell of joy greeted it. It played up and down the battle like a living flame, rapid and irresistible. It danced through the forwards and flickered round the goal. In the heart of each Corinthian new life and courage glowed. Like soldiers under Napoleon's eye, each did the impossible. Benjie had come, and Benjie was victory.

As the third shout of joy went up from Corinth, and the game drew even, a deeper voice was heard through the air, crying, "Brayvo, Benjie!" All looked round, and part of a brown face was seen peering through that hole in the shed's tiling, but was withdrawn as soon as seen. "Blest if it bain't old gaffer Abram!" they said, laughing. "He's scrabbled oop to get a sight on our Benjie."

When the match came to an end at last, owing to the dispersion of the ball's stuffing, and the Corinthians had cheered the Allcomers, and left the field with the sweet sense of weariness glorified by victory, Benjie found his father doubled over a book beside the furnace. He was reading his favourite story—the life and death of Samson.

"Benjie," he said, as he stirred up the smouldering coals, "don't be pooffed oop more nor what's convenient."

"I bain't pooffed oop," said Benjie, mounting the treadle.

"No, nor Samson wasn't to be called pooffed oop neither, so far as I make out. He just took things as they came—lions, or gates, or Philistines, or Delilahs. But he was made to be a warnin' to men like me and the man as you'll grow to."

Benjie said nothing, but he perceived that his father's mind was strangely excited, for as he worked he kept singing his favourite verse, beginning:

> "For me, a clod of living earth,
>   I glorify Thy name."

And when, at the half-hour allowed for tea, they sat drinking out of the same mug, and his father missed two of his lawful turns without noticing it, Benjie wondered what might be coming next.

"I can't read nothink to forbid me thinkin'," said Abram at last, "but it must 'ave been a grand moment when Samson felt them pillars go crack, and 'eard the Philistines start laughin' t'other side their mouths. Once on a time I'd a grand moment same as that myself. Yes, it was grand, but no doubt ensnarin'. It came through me being a rare joomper with the weights, for all you'd never think it."

"I've 'eard tell on yer as such," said Benjie.

"Yer 'ave?" cried Abram, drawing up his head, whilst his eyes grew bright. "When I was twenty, people came from as far as Walsall to see me joomp; and I've 'eard a many say it was well worth the money spent in drinks and rail. I was a part of the Whitsun feets. I don't speak with vainglory, seein' I'm not to be called the same man no longer now—hardly."

He was silent for a time, and then suddenly

continued: "It was maybe a year after I'd give oop diversion as bein' unprofitable. I was walkin' one evenin' across that same Cop out there, where you was playin' just now, and I see by the crowd and the passage down the middle that they was at the joompin' still. And one on 'em catches sight on me. It was Coaly Taylor, and he was reckoned a good joomper since I'd give oop. So he calls to me to coom and show how it was done; and with that he looks round and laughs a bit scornful.

"'I've 'eard you don't want no showin',' says I, speakin' him civil.

"'Don't you know Abram can't joomp no more since he was took soft?' says Susie Bowler, who was standin' and holdin' Coaly's coat, and lookin' very conformable in a lilac cotton.

"'Yes,' says somebody, 'he's give oop his joompin' and his gal, and we all know who's took 'em both on.'

"At that everybody starts loffing, and Susie turns very white, and Coaly takes off 'is cap, and makes as if bowin' to thank me.

"'Well,' I says, strippin' off my outer clothes, 'I don't mind tryin' again just for old sakes.'

"So I took the weights, and fixed my heels tight together, and swung my arms to get the lift, and I joomped—once—twice—and just when I'd ought to have joomped thrice and dropped the weights, a summat came over my sperrit, and I stood gapin' like a silly.

"The people kind of groaned, and some starts callin' out, and some says, 'Poor old Piety!' But lookin' round, I see I'd stopped close agen Susie's lilac dress, and I catch 'er lookin' at me, not loffin', nor yet pityin', but with a look I never see afore. So I says, 'Stick up a chair;' and I take my two leaps, and over that chair I go, same as if flyin'. So I says, 'Stick up another;' and I went on joompin' easy as a cat till we'd got oop to six chairs in a row. Then they called on Coaly to joomp, and he cleared the six, for he was a fine joomper, but I knowed he'd never cleared more nor seven. So I says, 'Stick on two at a time,' and over them eight I went. But Coaly, seein' it, puts on his clothes, and snails away. So I says, 'Stick on two more.' Then I grip the weights and plant my feet, and the people never breathed. Two leaps I take with the swing, and then I joomp and throw down the weights, and over them ten chairs I go, for all the world the same as any flea, if I may say it without vain boastin'.

"They made a fine to-do over me, did the people; and Susie stood outside of them, red as fire, with her eyes full of water, and her mind unsettled if to laugh or cry.

"Well, you was born about a year after that joomp, and uncommon proud Susie was of you so long as she kept livin'. Too proud maybe of both on us she was, and that's likely the reason she had bad luck with the second. Anyways, my pride was sore humbled when she died. And now, sooner than see you fall into my temptations, I'd choose for summat to happen to you to prevent it. But after all you're noways likely to grow so strong as me, that being summat extry. So now turn on the blast again."

Bellows and hammer renewed their monotonous symphony. Hour after hour, quite hidden in the darkness himself, Benjie stared down upon the dull-red scene, as step by step the process was continuously repeated—the great iron rod thrust into the furnace till it glowed, the end rapidly measured off on the gauge, bent on the suage, cut over the hardy, plunged again into the furnace, drawn out white and sparkling by the dog, hooked on to the last link, which still showed a sullen crimson, laid on the bicken, and welded with great blows from the oliver whilst the living iron, white as hoar-frost, splashed and spurtled round like water; and all the time the treadle creaked, and the blast went panting through the gleeds.

But as the cable slowly grew, Benjie could not make out what was happening to the old place. It no longer seemed the same. His father was growing into such a queer-looking giant, and the boy could not imagine what kind of giant's food he was cooking so diligently at the fire. He tried to keep thinking over the glories of the afternoon, but the memory of the match seemed to float away from his mind. He clung heavily to the chains, and every few minutes he changed his foot on the treadle. Towards midnight the giant seemed to swell with a peculiar exaltation, and began singing strange hymns. At last Benjie heard him cry out: "Stick to it, lad! Ten more links and it's doon, and no breakin' in upon the Sabbath.

There's no two men in the coontry could have got through such a bit of work. Not as we must count that for righteousness."

"I bain't countin' it," said Benjie, and let go the chains, and just rolled from the treadle in a helpless lump on to the sharp edges of old iron and coals and boards beneath. "Put me to play in goal," he said; and Abram took him in his arms and carried him into the house.

"Is he goin' to die straight off?" the father asked when morning dawned again, and the doctor was still watching, though he had done all he could.

"Of course not. I am afraid this leg'll be a bit crippled, but that's all."

"Crippled?" said Abram, sitting down suddenly on the edge of the bed. "A son of me a cripple?"

"Don't thee take on so," said Benjie; "we can work the blast with arms in place of feet."

"It bain't the blast I'm thinkin' on," said the father.

"And if it came to the very worst, a boy can go to heaven as well on one leg as on two," said the doctor, knowing the man, and only anxious to give comfort.

THE OLD ADAM

"It bain't heaven I'm thinkin' on neither, God help me," said Abram, and great tears began to roll down his brown face. "It's his football I'm thinkin' on. It was only last afternoon, and there's the mud still stickin' to his trouseys. And now never no more!"

"I've been thinkin' on that too," said Benjie. "But it was only a diversion," he added, bursting into tears of sympathy.

VIII

AN AUTUMN CROCUS

AMONG the many Quixotic theories which thronged through Doctor Maguire's brain, there was one upon which he liked to insist with all his power of paradox. "We English, whom clever people think so stupid," he used to say, "are now confronted by three portents—the Jew, the Irish, and the poor. The Jew has been well called Jacob without the ladder; the others we may call Esau without the birthright, and Lazarus with a discriminating Charity Organisation Society's dog to lick his sores. Our ruin by these portents is only to be averted by the thing called love. Let Jew and Christian, Celt and Saxon, rich and poor, together join hand and heart in marriage, and in twenty-five years we shall have extinguished a cantankerous old ritual, a memory of blood and bailiffs, and the demon of hereditary inequality. Surely for such an object just one generation might consent to make love on first principles. We are harassed by the triple warfare. Now, in all history there has only been one war with an entirely satisfactory conclusion. It was the war with the Amazons, and it ended in the mutual embraces of the two armies engaged."

"Well," his friends would retort, "you are still a bachelor. Why don't you make a start yourself?"

"Yes," he answered gravely, "I am bound to do myself what I know to be the duty of every one. Some day I shall marry under the Categorical Imperative."

"It was as jolly under the mistletoe, or even under the rose," they would answer. And then, if they were very old friends, they would suddenly be silent or change the subject, remembering a vague rumour of some love-story in which the doctor had borne a Stoic's part without flinching, but had nevertheless fallen lamed out of the ranks of the rising young surgeons in London.

Doctor Maguire was not a man to draw back from his word. In the lonely evenings he brooded over his theory, following it out to its lowest practical issues. And in the day-time, as he went abroad upon his healing tasks, he would keep an astronomer's watch for the appearance of that being, surely not impossible, with whom he might conjoin for equality's furtherance. But as he looked upon the world of common air and labour, he often sighed, lamenting his lack of courage or of human sympathy. "'Il y a des hommes; il y a femme.' Yes, I know," he would reflect. "Every man worthy of the human name loves all women. And yet, might there not be one, or two, or three, possessing some quality which might precipitate a random and diffused affection, giving to love that further element which Arnold defined by his word, the eternal? These piteous conscripts of labour in the work-yards, deformed, sore-eyed, sexless, and wasted—is it possible to take one of them to my heart on first principles and call her my eternal? It is true, as the poet says:

> "Care-bit, erased,
> Broken-up beauties ever took my taste
> Supremely."

There is comfort in the words. But after

all, the poet did not wed some toiling child of poor humanity, but a mere poetess."

Full of these thoughts, and a little saddened by the naked hideousness of things as they are, the doctor was returning from a rather distant visit one afternoon towards his lonely hermitage or outpost, at Wenley. It was a lovely November day. A boisterous wind came storming straight from distant Wales and the pure western hills. The windows of the mining villages along the ridges to the north, flashed and sparkled in the low autumn sun. There was a sense of warm relaxation, of release in all the air, as though, out of due season, the old Earth felt in her stagnant blood the thrill of spring. As he ranged along, letting the wind and sun play on his grizzled hair, the doctor discovered a narrow footpath, unknown to him, but obviously a short cut. It led across a wide region of desert, known as the Rough Heaps, the site of old mines and ironworks long since abandoned. Piled on the distorted surface, the ancient refuse-heaps rose almost like natural hills, though the grey boulders on their sides were seen to be nothing but circular masses of slag from the bottom of blast-furnaces long cold. Here and there stood the ruin of an engine-house with its broken column of chimney. But the wreckage of man's efforts was being slowly covered up and transformed —slowly, but as surely as if the wreck lay full fathom five. Among the boulders which had melted with fervent heat, along the old "breeze-bank" where women had sifted gleeds and "bull-dog" for the furnaces, even on the heaps of burnt dust and crumbled clay, sorrel was growing, and a few ox-eyes lingered, and hawk-weed and frugal broom. Among those artificial rocks, where, side by side with "clodhoppers" and pipits, they had made their nests last spring, a few pied wagtails had remained to brave the winter, and as the doctor passed they bobbed and flirted at him with a grey and white frivolity.

"Here too," he cried with joy—"even here Nature is at work and is doing her best. How I adore you, worthy old girl!"

Suddenly he paused, beholding before him the figure of a girl in the flesh, worthy perhaps as Nature, but not as old. She stood within the doorway of a ramshackle white cottage, one storey high, apparently the only human shelter left in the wide desolation. Without pause she laboured at the forging of a chain, and as her little hammer fell upon the links and made the shining iron splash, she was singing to herself for joy. Her voice came beating up against the wind, and the doctor caught the well-known tune and words:

> "The King of love my shepherd is,
> Whose goodness faileth never;
> I nothing lack if I am His."

"Hymns," he reflected, after his manner, "are now the love-songs of the English people. It is of love she sings, and she thinks it is religion. How she stands there, glowing in the orange of sunlight and the crimson of the furnace! Is she not like her who would have been invisible in fire, so bright with love she glowed?"

He drew nearer, treading softly as in an enchanted region, though the hammer and the roar of the blast prevented his footsteps from being heard, and the girl appeared to be possessed by the zeal of work. Alone, and singing in such a place as that, she seemed almost a fairy being which a child might come upon in haunted lands. But she was only a common chain-maker, adding link to link. And her main garment was a great sacking apron, carefully arranged to cover the fragments of a light print frock, and gathered loosely in at the waist with a rope. Suddenly, after a final blow on a dull-red link slowly cooling upon the anvil, she threw her head back, and passed her hand over her wet forehead and neck; and still from her full brown throat poured the song :

"And oh, what rapture of delight
From His pure chalice——"

Then the light brown eyes, set in the clearest white, rested upon the doctor so close at hand. Instantly the singing stopped, and there was a great silence, as when a lark falls home to the ground. In her look there was no trace of fear; but unconcerned gravity and the sweetness of welcome contended there.

"You seem to like the work," said the doctor absurdly.

"It helps to pass the time away a bit," she answered at once; and the doctor recognised the formula in which many find so strange a consolation for a life of almost ceaseless toil.

AN AUTUMN CROCUS

"What are the chains used for?" he asked.

"The rigging for fishing-boats, they tell me," she said.

"Then you have the lives of men in your hands."

"As far as chains go, they've got no cause to fear for their bodies sinking to the bottom," she said, with a laugh. "My work's true, same as God's above."

"It must be bad out here in winter," said the doctor, feeling sadly like an amateur interviewer, but unable to turn his eyes away from her.

"Dear, no!" she answered, going on with the work. "Winter's good for the likes of we. It stops the sweat runnin'. Yes, I'm at it all the year round, but for Sundays and bank holidays. I'm sure I dunno what the poor 'ud do for a holiday, if it wasn't for the Sundays, and Jesus bein' born and dyin' and rising up again."

"But aren't you lonely out here by yourself?"

"You can't be lonely if you've got Jesus and the saints with you."

"So you're a Catholic?"

"Dear, no! I don't trouble my head nothing

K

about that," she answered, with her sudden smile, thrusting a new rod into the blast. "Mother used to talk about the saints, and I've kep' 'em up. It seems to make more of Them above. Sounds kind of friendly, don't you think? You see, I'm an orphing, working mostly alone, but for Them; and then there's *him* over there mostly hangin' about too. We're both orphings, me and Willie."

The doctor looked in the direction of her nod, and discovered the figure of a boy or young man sitting motionless under the brow of the rugged hillside across the path, and watching him intently. He was hardly to be distinguished among the greys and browns of the refuse and grasses.

"Oh, that's your brother, is it?" he asked quickly.

"He's a pretty sort of brother, is Willie!" she cried, laughing, but not unkindly. "I often tell him he ought to have been born a gentleman, because he's good for pretty nearly everything but doin' work."

"Oh, he's as idle as a gentleman, is he?" said the doctor, a little vexed at such a definition, in spite of his Socialism.

"Oh, come now," she answered, in a relenting voice, "he isn't quite so bad as what that comes to. Two days a week he gets a bit of gamblin' to do, and he's a rare hand at catchin' a rabbit after sundown. Why, what do you think he's doing there now? Ever since his breakfast he's been watchin' a bit of a net he's stuck up on the rocks for the birds. He'll be as happy as a lark if he brings in a poor little mouthful of a thing to supper not enough for one, feathers and all. No; he isn't exackly to be called idle, isn't Willie. But them's the sort of things a gentleman might do just as well. To say nothing of fightin'. He's grand at fightin' too. You should just see him strip."

She paused in her hammering for a moment, drawing herself up, and gazing at the distant figure with eyes full of joyful admiration.

"Just like that," thought the doctor, "a Spartan girl must have gazed upon her athlete brother starting naked for the race."

"Yes, Willie's grand, and no mistake," she murmured. "He'd have done first-rate for a gentleman. And somehow I always did think I'd have a kind of fancy to be a lady too."

She turned again to her work, and the doctor

watched the unerring hands moving to and fro. When at last he said good-night, and turned along the track for home, he saw that strange figure on the opposite bank still sitting silent and motionless, except that, without any movement of the eyes, his head turned slowly to follow the stranger's course.

All that night the doctor felt a dizziness and exaltation of mind, like a man who, after long years of sea or plain, climbs a mountain-top, and is bewildered at the sense of space.

Next day and the next he visited that distant patient beyond the Rough Heaps again. He was tenderly careful of all his cases, but for that case he seemed to feel an almost excessive solicitude, and the path across the waste was certainly very convenient. To the doctor it was more. There was about the scene a touch of wild beauty, of romance even, in contrast to those common Midland surroundings. It seemed an earnest of what all England's hell-holes would become in another century. Or did it owe its peculiar colour to a certain smile, a look of welcome, a shrewd or startling word? or to that wild figure of a man, visible for a moment as he lurked behind a mass of slag, and just showed a head above the steep bank before he vanished silently as a mountain goat? Twice indeed, when the night had already closed in, the doctor found the girl still at her work, but apparently alone. Willie was away—"gone to his bed," she supposed, or out in the country on business. Then she laughed her sweet low laugh; and the doctor could not help picturing that untamed brother of hers as some Faun revelling in woods among the furry animals which he loved and slaughtered.

So passed the full-orbed days—nearly three weeks of them. Each bathed in gold they seemed, in spite of November's rains and fog. Then came a Sunday when, as the doctor turned into the familiar little path, he sighed to think that nothing could now prevent his outlying patient's speedy convalescence. Still his mind was full of delicate pleasure, and as he approached the lonely hut he was repeating to himself the lines:

> "Is it a lark I hear?
> Over the firmament thin clouds are wild,
> And autumn's afternoon on roadsides drear
>   Scatters the clammy leaves.
> Dear lark, that sang when summer was a child,
> The fields are empty of their summer sheaves;
>   Why tell of spring to the declining year?"

Suddenly he was aware of a confused noise, the trampling and shouts of battle, and running to the top of a mound, he beheld a scene of conflict which in calmer moments he might have called a grimy epic. In a hollow not far away was gathered a dingy knot of colliers and pallid factory-hands, such as are wont in remote corners to beguile the Day of Rest with pitch-and-toss. But no longer now were they standing in concentric rings, with heads squeezed together over the issues of fate. A confused and shifting mob, rolling curses to the wintry sky, they were closing savagely in upon some object of their wrath. Yelping like terriers disappointed of their rat, some kept running round the outskirts of the fray, or strove to scramble over the shoulders of the foremost ranks. But in the centre the random blows fell as thick as on a threshing-floor where four men swing the loosely-jointed flails, and through the wide-open door the dusty labour hums. With his back against a bit of ruined wall stood Willie, and the girl was close beside him. They were alone, and hard pressed, having scarcely room to move. Once and again the doctor saw the length of a brown arm shoot

AN AUTUMN CROCUS

out straight in the enemy's face. Twice he saw the girl raise a heavy iron rod, and strike; and as she struck he saw her laugh. But the end was come. Almost before the doctor could realise the scene, a crashing blow took Willie full in the throat. With a gasp he fell where he stood, his limbs curling under him. Seeing him disappear, the wild mouths raised a yell of triumph, and then the ignoble crowd held off a little, like journalists when a statesman falls. With one great cry the girl strode across the body, and swinging her iron rod clear round the small half-circle, she beat them further back by the mere terror of her fury.

"Do for the witch too! Send 'em below together!" shouted voices from the edge of the crowd. A hand was thrust out. It clutched her tattered dress at the throat, and rent it open. Down came the iron rod, and she laughed again. At that moment the doctor charged from the rear; around his head his folded umbrella made horrid circles. He shouted as he had read a soldier shouts. And as the Russian columns gave and shook when charged by the British line, so the serried gamblers gave and shook. Some one cried,

"Police!" They opened out and broke. They vanished over the hills. Almost without a blow the doctor held the field.

The girl still stood astride the fallen body. Over one shoulder a wild coil of hair hung down, and there was blood upon her neck. She drew her breath hard, and laughed. Her whole body trembled with ferocity, and the joy of battle shone in her face.

"Cowards!" she cried amongst other wilder words, as she wiped the foam from her mouth with the back of her hand. "Oh, you cowards, you dirty, mopin' shop-boys and machiners, call yourselves men?—you accidents of creation! I'd make men as good as you in my back garden with a bit of dirt. To set on my Willie, thirty of you together, just for being cleverer than any factory spawn like you'll ever be. Win? What's the good of being a man if he couldn't win off stuff like you? He's likely always to win, I should hope! But there's five of you I've marked. There's five of you won't move comfortable yet awhile, that's sure. Yes, there you go, runnin' back to your holes; and when you get there, may you be hungry by day and cold by night! may you hate your wives, and never know a woman's love! may your children laugh at your grey hairs, and nobody stand by when the earth falls on your coffins, and nobody give you another thought for ever and ever!"

Her voice had risen to the impassioned cry which marks the wilder-blooded race. The iron rod was stretched out towards the line of the foe's retreat. That word "witch" came into the doctor's mind; but he had already turned, as a doctor should, to the man on the ground. The shoulders were partly supported by the wall, but the head was tilted helplessly forward, and a thin line of blood trickled from the mouth.

"Help me to carry him," said the doctor. Instantly she was on her knees, and began passionately to kiss the green unconscious face all over, and to wipe off the blood with her rag of a handkerchief, calling him by every endearing name. But he gave no sign of life. His hands lay half closed and senseless upon the grass.

Between them they carried him slowly into the cottage. "Here, on my own bed," she said, and opened a door leading out of the forge into a tiny white-washed room. Except a narrow iron bed, a scrap of looking-glass, and the seat of a broken chair with half a comb lying on it, there was no furniture of any kind. They laid the body on the torn and dingy coverlet of ancient patchwork, and opened the blue shirt at the neck and chest. Anxious and busy with his healing art as the doctor was, he could not help noticing the beauty of the form, so hard and thin and woodland.

"No, I haven't got no brandy nor nothing," the girl said, in answer to his question. "Oh, doctor dear, what shall us do?"

"There, there, my dear," he answered. "He'll be all right. The bleeding seems to have stopped. We've only got to chafe his skin now and get him warm again."

For warmth, she laid the warmth of her own body against him. For chafing, she kissed his heart till the skin was red. She opened his mouth and put her own to it, as though her breath must needs bring back his life. And from time to time the doctor could not avoid overhearing snatches of muttered but passionate prayer.

"O Lord, save Willie," she kept repeating.

"Save him, and I'll tell him it ain't right for him always to be winning. You see, he can't help winning, he's so clever. But I know it isn't right. Save him, O Lord, and I'll do double work to keep him fed. I've been a good girl up to now. I've done all I could think of to please you. But you must save my Willie. My name's set down in your book, I know. You must save Willie, O Lord, or you may blot my name out of your book for ever. Me and Willie count for one."

Still the body remained ghastly and unconscious. She began to cry. The tears fell warm on the young man's breast, and she wiped them with her hair.

"O Jesus darlin'," she sobbed, "save Willie, 'cos I love him so."

She knelt upon the bed, and took the man by the shoulders and shook him. "Willie, Willie!" she cried. "Rousel up, man! you can't be dyin'. Rousel up, I tell thee!"

He opened his eyes and looked at her quietly. She moved no more than if she had seen the dead return to life.

"Flo," he whispered, "did they nail the tin?"

"Not them," she said.

"Flo," he went on, "you be worthy of me. You've got a heart like a tiger."

She caught his hand to her breast, laughing for pleasure. Suddenly he became aware of the doctor's presence, and fixed his eyes on him with the furtive restlessness of a cat watching a stranger in the room. The doctor laid a hand soothingly on his arm; but he shrank away in terror, and clutched at the girl's skirt like a child.

"Flo," he said, "he's coom to take thee away from me. I knowed it from the first; I seed his breathin' stop whiles he looked on you that first time he came. Don't you leave me, Flo. You surely ain't goin' to leave me at the end of it all?"

"Don't you be talking of such things," she answered. "Nobody's going to take me away. You lay still in my nice bed where you be, and we'll put you straight, and then I'll send the gentleman off. No offence, sir," she added; "but Willie's always a bit shy before strangers. He don't mean no harm."

Very tenderly she undressed him, brought water in a zinc pail, tore a handful of soft stuff out of a new mop-head, and with it bathed the bruised face and blood-stained mouth. Then she spread the grey bedclothes over him, and smoothed them down. The doctor gave his final directions, and looked thoughtfully at the patient again. "It is an interesting and uncommon type," he said to himself. "Some people would call it pagan. Properly speaking it is the normal man—a thing so rare that English civilisation can make no use of it, but as a literary curiosity."

He followed the girl out into her workshop, and down the rough piece of garden, encircled by a ring of elder hedge. The sun had set, but the sky was strangely clear, and in the pale yellow light above the west the young moon stood naked and seemed to tremble. Here and there a great star hung down from the depths of the air, and looked closer than usual to the beloved little earth. Jagged edges of rock and branches of gorse stood out brown and purple against the fading light. The girl was leaning beside a post where the gate ought to have been. Idealised by the night, she seemed a wild spirit in pallid robes, as tender as the moon.

"Good-night," said the doctor, taking her

hand, and remembering with a thrill of passionate sympathy all that was signified by its hardness. "Good-night. I suppose I must not stop any longer, though I should like to. I think your brother will go on well now."

"My brother? Oh, you mean Willie," she said, with her little laugh. "He isn't my brother, thank God. He's nothing but an orphing I've been lookin' after, because he ran away from his step-father when his mother got married. So he took to living like a rat in one of those old engine-houses up there, and one night he comes to my door by the bicken as starved as a cade lamb. So, me being an orphing same as him, it comes into my head to do for him a bit, because he was so helpless. That's all—I mean that's what Willie is."

"That's all. To be sure. Of course. Yes. I quite understand," stammered the poor doctor with more than usual ineptitude.

"No, that isn't all neither," she said, first glancing aside, and then looking him in the face with a kind of defiance, and drawing her hand away. "That isn't all, because Willie's my lover—my own lover. We've been loving each other near on four months now, and for the last three weeks I've only been waiting for the work to give me a spare day to be married."

"I suppose you've had your bans published, then?" said the doctor, with a sickening feeling that he was like a churchwarden giving good advice to Artemis and Endymion.

"Bands?" she said, looking absently at the virgin moon. "What's them? Oh yes, a course there's the bands of marriage. I had pretty nigh forgot them, and they'll have to hurry up a bit now that I've taken Willie into my own house at last. But I'm only thinking over what he said. Did you hear him tell me I'd got the heart of a tiger? Wasn't that sweet? He isn't given to sayin' much, isn't Willie; but when it comes it's worth the waitin' for—same as love."

"Yes," he said, in his hearty, laughing voice, "love is well worth waiting for, I suppose. Good-bye now, as they say over there in Wales."

"Good-bye," she answered. "You'll be passing to-morrow as usual, and will look in on Willie?"

"No; but I'll write to a friend to take up the case. I shan't be coming this way again."

Do what he would, he couldn't keep his voice quite up to the level pitch.

"Why, what's the matter?" she said, catching his hand in both of hers. "Why can't you come again? I haven't even said thank you yet. What's the matter with you?"

"Nothing," he said—"nothing at all. Good-bye."

But she clung to him still, and looked earnestly in his face. They stood quite still, and as she looked he saw the sign of understanding come into her eyes. He was terribly afraid she was going to cry. She came a step nearer to him, and put up her face as though to see more clearly in the moon's thin light. His strong will rocked and swayed.

"Could you have——?" he whispered.

"I don't know," she said aloud. "I think I could. I do love you very much."

"As much as Willie?" he said, with a very poor attempt at a smile.

She looked at him steadily in silence, for a long time, as it seemed. Then almost imperceptibly he felt her draw a little backwards.

Suddenly she put her hands round his neck and drew his face down to hers.

"Good-night!" she said. "Good-night! Good-bye! Good-bye again!" and between each word she kissed him.

Next moment she was gone, and she shut the cottage door without even turning round.

That night Doctor Maguire made some random notes in a diary, which he kept partly for business, partly for the soothing consolation of rhetoric. Under heading "Sunday, Nov. 25," he wrote: "(1) Visited John Davidson, 'setter on' in No. 10 Pit, *ut supra;* convalescent; ordered tonics and good diet. Know he can't get either. *Mem.*, to send half-dozen Taragona, half bottle at a time, and label it as medicine, or else the whole family will tonic themselves. (2) Accident on Rough Heaps: severe blow on larynx; hæmorrhage slight; but prolonged syncope from shock to brain and nervous system. Treatment normal, but noticed beneficial result of warm stimulation and friction over the cardiac region. Patient would be of value to a sculptor or anatomist. Commended case to Dr. Weston of Sedgeley. Enclosed fee for special marriage license,

L

apparently desired by the patient. Wondered if it was not a waste of money.

"(3) In a cottage garden I observed a specimen of the autumn crocus, pale and pinkish, such as now covers the mountain pastures in the South. The Germans call it *Herbst Zeitlose*—the untimely flower of declining years.

"I notice that for three weeks I have forgotten all about first principles and my gospel of social regeneration. Mommsen is quite right: the world belongs not to reason, but to passion.

"Passion does not necessarily contradict reason; it supersedes reason; it vitalises reason.

"I also was quite right: in passion alone there is equality. Pater speaks nobly of 'the aristocracy of passion;' but he might just as well have said the democracy of passion.

"The second time! To see again the beatific vision—to feel the old throb, the old transfiguration of self and the world—to watch it all crumble into common dust, like a beloved saint's body! I who could love a dog, a rat—shall I not find one human heart that will let me love it and give me love for love?

"Renounce, say the wise. And we are tempted to cry in answer, 'O Renunciation, Renunciation, what crimes are committed in thy name!'

"But I gave up what never could have been mine. That is not even renunciation.

"'He who loves God has no right to ask that God should love him in return.' Brave old Spinoza! To love—how much more necessary it is than to be loved!

"And so to bed, as Pepys would say. For sheets I wrap myself in my own virtue—a chilly covering, to be sure.

"'O Hercules, what a cold bath!' cried the sun-browned savage in the Roman dungeon. Yes, the Roman dungeon of Stoicism is a cold bath.

"Well, I have taken my cold bath through all the winter of my life, and I hope to continue that sanitary practice to the end."

IX

MISS RACHEL

FROM time to time, for a long year past, the toil-encrusted hearts of Wenley had been stirred by rumours of the great disaster which had laid a hand like death's upon Kinestead, that pleasant village, only ten miles away, under those pale hills in the west. From time to time they did what they could to help. Themselves in misery's school had learnt to give succour. The hollow-cheeked collectors for the Kinestead Relief Fund, tramping far and wide through the country with their soiled little account-books, were always sure of scraping up a few pence at Wenley-on-the-Hill; and if they could sit awhile, they got a jug of beer; and even to supply them with food, courteous wit would elaborate some veiled device. Drink could always be given; but to give food without offence to the starving was a delicate matter. The donor, as a matter of course, had to consume a like amount himself; and if the rest of the company could be instructed to declare themselves just famishing for bread and cheese, the artifice was regarded as particularly successful. When once, under this solemn pretence, the wanderers had settled down into some kind of comfort, discreet questions would begin, and bit by bit the tale of all the woe would be unravelled. The prelude to the story, introduced with historic rather than poetic instinct, was the episode of Miss Rachel Redford, on whose so seeming-innocent head the blame for all the suffering was laid.

The Kinestead children, whose only idea of maternity was its age, always called her Mother Rachel; but she herself was rather precise in refusing even the title of Missis, which the neighbours would have allowed her in consideration of her gentle manners. In outward appearance she was as typical an old maid as ever rubbed her cat's feet on the door-mat, or surreptitiously passed her finger along the top of her friends' picture-frames and looked at it to test their cleanliness. A trim little body she was still, active and shapely, with sweet blue eyes, and a delicate little face, which flushed a maiden pink for sorrow at the sight of sorrow, and for shame at a word of shame. She was always scrupulously dressed in soft and well-fitting black; and on her neat brown hair she wore the pure and ghostly semblance of a widow's cap, as though in astral mourning for some husband who was never hers. In the ten years since she had first appeared at Kinestead from some northern county, her whitewashed cottage had grown after the image of herself, and seemed to stand apart from the rest of the red-brick row with a certain superfluity of daintiness. The white little "valence blind" across the bedroom window was shyly tied back in the middle with pale blue ribbons, as was at that time the superior mode. In the strip of garden scarcely a leaf was left awry. Tall virgin lilies grew there in June, thrown into purer relief by the purple heart's-ease along the window-ledge. A bishop had admired them. It was indeed observed that there was a want of variety in Miss Rachel's taste; but she herself did not hold with women who tire of a choice once made, flitting like mere moles from flower to flower of life. In the sitting-room lay six bound books of peaceful devotion and gardening, arranged like the spokes of a wheel round the axle-tree of a Bible, and carefully dusted every morning. Miss Rachel also possessed an old copy of a Family Byron, but it was kept under lock and key in a cupboard with the sugar, tea, and cruet-stand. In her kitchen, meat was never seen. She could not endure the sight of its redness or the smell of its cooking. Every Sunday she paid her neighbour sixpence for a hot cut from the joint, but it was supposed she gave it to the cat. It was well known that upstairs she had a bath.

A letter from America came for her about once a quarter, and she always sent the stamps up to the rectory, as a present to the young masters, with Miss Redford's compliments. She had a relation in America—a brother no doubt, for he bore the same name. He sent her money. The post-office people knew all about it. She had no cause to work. She was almost entitled to the respect due to independent means. That she had remained unmarried was in itself a proof of connection with the superior class which can afford a certain discrimination in the matter of husband or wife, and does afford it. No wonder that the shops where she dealt called her genteel, and the others "stand-offish." Yet she did in fact work every day, and worked hard, cutting out and fitting and sewing with her own fingers, much disdaining the dizzy and feverish machine. It was noticed, too, that she would only work in white stuffs, and hardly ever undertook an order except for little scraps of things such as "usen babies all"—so the children's carol says. It was a maidish peculiarity, and aroused ironic laughter among the Kinestead mothers, to whom another baby counted for rather less than another winter.

So unvarying were Miss Rachel's habits, so sensitive her repugnance to all the tarnish and soilure of this world, that gossip could scarcely believe its own tongue when it told how Miss Rachel had received Cissy Wilson into house and home—Cissy Wilson with her misfortune. And when the misfortune died, and Cissy, in accordance with the moral code, could return to her father's house and still not despair of a husband, gossip further repeated with pitying smiles that Miss Rachel had held that dead little image of a man in her arms, and talked to it motherly, and cried ever so, till at last the rector's gardener had to take it from her and carry it away for burial, like a superfluous kitten. But after that, Miss Rachel returned to her serene and cloistral ways, and nothing further occurred to draw on her the breath of applause or calumny. Had she been the ghost of a nun, her life could hardly have glided on with more unsullied course. She had become a standard and example in the village—a little difficult to live up to, perhaps, like a thin saint of old. But God is merciful; and we have not all the same gifts. So for the most part Miss Rachel was admired and favoured as a set-off to the more humane grossness of the many.

But there came a summer afternoon, and with it a stranger, big and sunburnt, a man of twenty-five or something more, having a short brown beard, and a way of moving his great shoulders loosely as he walked, like a mastiff. It was Sunday, and the quiet street which curled between the river and the hill was just awaking from the torpor of the Sabbath meal. The children were doddering past to Sunday school, and the girls half turned round to stare and titter. Now and again the stranger smiled as with distant remembrance of similar scenes. Loiterers at corners, and fathers leaning in their Sunday shirt sleeves from windows watched him at leisure down the whole length of the street. His hat was certainly broader in the brim than is needful in a land where for half the year the sun shrinks like the pupil of a cat's eye exposed to light. There was something sunny, too, about his whole bearing, a palpable happiness which betrayed an un-English habit of soul. Habitual joy was in his voice when he stopped to ask a question. So he lounged carelessly along, observing everything, delighting in everything, till he came opposite Miss Rachel's door. And then (oh, impious intrusion and desecration!) he turned and jumped the neat white gate—jumped it clean, instead of fumbling at the latch, and landed with a splash of little stones upon the virginal garden path.

"Oh, my!" cried all the village. "Won't Miss Rachel be in a stew over her nice gravel!"

But worse remained behind. He strode up to the painted blue door, and kicked at it with his heavy boot. The village was dumb.

"Mrs. Redford live here?" he shouted, in a voice like a cavalry trumpet.

The window-blind in the upper chamber was seen to flutter, and through the open window came the reply: "No—yes—I mean I am Miss Redford, if you please, sir."

"I reckon that's all the same," said the stranger, and walked straight into the house, slamming the door hard behind him—"enough to bang poor Miss Rachel to bits," said the village.

Then the people in the next house heard her clear and delicate tones calling down the stairs: "If you wish to speak to me, sir, would you kindly rub the dust from your boots, and take a seat in the front room. I will come down in a few minutes." From which they rightly concluded that Miss Rachel had gone upstairs to "clean herself."

Listening intently, they heard her light and dainty footstep descend. "To what, sir, may I owe the honour——?" Her voice was a little nervous perhaps.

"Oh, tell me!—have you news—news of him?" she said, speaking strangely and quick.

A fine deep laugh was the answer.

"Richard! O Richard!" came a woman's cry, and for what more the neighbours heard, they could find no satisfactory interpretation. Only, the old grandmother, who, in spite of summer, was cowering over the fire to warm the blood in the great black veins of her skinny hands, suddenly spoke for the first time that day, and said: "Is that a loover Miss Rachel's got in there? So her's got un at last, has she? and why not, I'd like to know? Her ain't old. I know the meanin' of that kind of voice. Her's got un, you may lay yer life. Leastways, it's either a loover or a baby her's got, that I'll swear to, and I s'pose the loover's most likely." Then she laughed and chuckled to herself over sweet old memories till she almost coughed herself to death.

Later on they heard Miss Rachel setting out her tea things. The milkman called. It was one of her "stand-offish" offences that unlike her level Christians she had milk every day. But this afternoon she asked for a pennyworth of cream beside! To the chemist down the street the milkman expressed his opinion that Miss Rachel was "launchin' out."

"Seein' as summut extryordinar must have 'appened," he went on, with the justifiable self-importance of a society journalist who is snuffing round some problem of sex, "I just took the liberty to peep in at the winder, whiles Miss Rachel had gone to fetch a joog. And there in the parlour—oh deary me! what ever do yer think I seed? Why, that great lumpin' thing of a man was settin' on the sofy with all his legs sprawdlin' about the room. And he'd got a great brown cigar stuck in his mouth, and —well, you know Miss Rachel, how she rucks up her little snoffle at the first smell of a nice clean bit of baccy, same as if it was the devil's brimstone-and-treacle set alight to from below! And up in the cage by the ceiling I heard that yaller dicky-bird of hern give a kind of tweet, most despairin', as if it was just goin' off into a faint—and no wonder, neither, at such carryin's on—of a Sunday too!"

The six bells in the old church at the top of the steep green hill above the village, set about their weekly problem of proving into how many combinations they could arrange themselves. Miss Rachel's door opened and she looked out. But seeing an acquaintance stare at her in going by, she drew back, and in the kindly shelter of the passage she laid her face against the stranger's coat. "They shall never know, shall they, Richard? Never!" she said.

"I don't see that it matters much," he answered.

"For my sake," she whispered.

"Never," he said, and tenderly laid his great hand on the flushed face turned up to him with closed eyes.

They went out together into the brilliant evening sunlight, and down the dusty street. The eyes of all the world glared upon them. She slid her hand through his arm. In a little while she withdrew it, and carefully watched the stones, as though they were things of new interest. As she approached the chapel, she felt that the whole congregation was moving towards the door very slowly, so as to miss nothing of their stare. She could not help seeing their feet and legs. Most were known to her. Those were Mr. Watson's boots. He was a deacon, and always walked on the outside of his feet to stifle the noise. On the outside of his feet he also swayed in time to the hymns. Those were Watty Benton's bare legs. She had made those embroidered drawers herself. That was Liza Meekin's red and purple stocking, hanging in loose rings all down her leg as usual—the slattern! Next came stout Mrs. Butler's "elastic sides," slit down the instep from top to toe; and old Gabriel's wooden leg; and little Florrie's green skirt, with the last tuck newly let down, showing the stuff's original glory of hue; and the armoured boots of Mr. Kerr the puddler, who never wore socks for fear of cold feet; and poor Gertrude's skirt sweeping the dust, though it had been doubled up inside by her mother's direction when she bequeathed it to her on the deathbed last week. And then came Cissy Wilson's trim ankles in the tiny low shoes. Miss Rachel knew them well enough.

All went by at slow march as in a Georgian review. She breathed more freely when the line was finished. She longed to be back behind the shelter of her own door, yet a strange sense of proud elation drove her on, and, as she turned up the steep pathway to the church, she ventured to cast sidelong glances at the few acquaintances who were also climbing the hill. They saluted her with respect, but there was a shyness, a silent difference in their look, which made her blood flame. She had herself sometimes felt that shyness on meeting a girl with her lover in a lane alone. When at last the churchyard wall was reached, she stopped and looked back. The cheery old village with its broad street of red and white gables lay far below. The fruit gardens of the larger houses straggled a little way up the hill. Beyond the street the slow river drew its arc, nearly hidden by willows; and beyond the river ran the straight line of a canal, telling of far-off estuaries and seas at either end. Around stood the low hills, heavy with summer woods—all but one which rose into clear air under the western sky, bare and sharp as an axe's edge, and seemed an alluring promise of mountains not so very far away. But over the north and east of the evening blue a great oppression of smoke from the Black Country brooded unmoved, and Miss Rachel pointed out to the stranger the ironworks hardly half a mile up the canal—the Nelson Works, sole cause of Kinestead's prosperity.

"Yes," he said. "I went round to have a look at them before I came to see you. They are an interesting relic of antiquity."

"But the village is pretty, isn't it?"

"Yes, it's pretty. I think I never saw a really finished town before. I'll take another look at it before I go."

"Oh, don't say go!" she cried, laying a hand quickly on his arm. They turned and entered the church together.

Miss Rachel, though a Quakeress by instinct and aspiration, cherished a girlish affection for that old church. She loved its quiet shades and the grey old stones. She loved it best in summer, when the evening light entered the open door under the tower, and sometimes a black-faced sheep, all golden in the sun, would peer in, and stamp its foot amazed. She loved the surplices, and the crimson hood and the white. Emblems of sin and innocence, she thought them; and it pleased her to observe that the young curate wore the sin, and the older man the innocence. She loved the cool peacefulness, the intervals of silence which broke the distant mutter of incomprehensible prayers, the faint mouldering smell of age which she supposed to arise from the clean and ancient bones of the dead. She loved the immaculate polish of the old brass eagle at the reading-desk, and the clasps and candlesticks on the altar, sparkling like very flames. And she loved the retirement of a little corner near the door, almost hidden from sight by a great round pillar. Unnoticed there, she could think and remember in peace.

But that night some unnamed spirit seemed to possess her. Instead of turning to her modest nook as usual, she found herself impudently marching straight up the nave, and entering the large pew in the very centre. Now, to the rector it was a matter for regretful sighs, to the curate a theme of passionate and prophetic objurgation, that the church had not yet been reseated. The old high pews still stood with all their dear memories of invisible but straight-backed slumber. At first sight they seemed to afford a pleasing variety by facing in every possible direction. Even the choir turned its back upon the altar, and a full congregation looked like a volunteer battalion which had tried to form square by half companies and lamentably failed. But in reality a kind of order reigned in the chaos; for every seat had been set to face towards that very pew which Miss Rachel and the stranger entered. Probably it had originally been the squire's pew, and the arrangement was a tribute of respect to him. For though equality before God's throne is indeed an acceptable doctrine, there is no need officiously to forestall the Day of Judgment. But perhaps some squire, at a loss for further security, had raised a mortgage on his plot of God's house, and the creditor had foreclosed. Anyhow, that pew was now as free as the rest, and the congregation that evening was grateful indeed for the arrangement of the seating, for owing to his position no movement of Miss Rachel's handsome stranger could be missed from any quarter of the church.

The service ran its wonted course. The kindly old rector preached to the winds, the tombstones, and the curate about the moral qualities typified by the various portions of Aaron's vestments. The people with great cheerfulness and spirit sang the sweet tune which told their longing to be at rest in Paradise with loyal hearts and true. Then all assembled in knots outside the porch, and the murmur of comment and speculation arose. There was no more exhilarating point of life than a summer hour after evening service, when the spirit returned, braced and dimly sanctified, to the old loves and uses of the earth.

"Yes, big, and very decent-looking too," said a critic on the one theme of interest. "But he didn't know his way about the prayers."

"Well, it do coom hard unless you've been trained to it young. They tell me it ain't the same abroad where he cooms from."

"It's worst in the mornings. Them Commandments and that Collect! Who'd ever have thought where to look for 'em? But it was the Psalms as put him off the scent to-night. And this curate don't even give out the day of the month. I'm wrong all week since he came."

"Well, it don't matter much about understandin' the Psalms since they took to singin' 'em."

"I caught Madge Overton having a look at 'im. Her's mighty stuck up since her went to the school from her aunt's in London."

"See Miss Rachel blushin', too, at standin' there alongside a young man!"

"Put her in mind of the one she wanted to have afore any of us was born, I reckon."

"Hear her sing 'My soul doth magnify'! Bold as brass. I caught the rector lookin'."

"That was the first time her climbed up and stood on the big bass—hassock some call it—so as him and her might lay hold on the same book side by side."

"Yes, her put me in mind of my white whippet hound alongside of a big Newfoundland dog."

"See her when they started readin' about Hannah makin' the little coat! I bobbed up, and down she slid into the pew, and I didn't quite like to lean over to look what she was doing."

"Her's got the leavin's of a pretty young woman, I must say. Colourin's been good, there's no denyin' it."

"Call *her* pretty? And as to colourin'!"

Purple bonnet-strings were thrown carelessly back, the further to reveal the exuberance and roseate warmth of nature in her copious prime.

"Hush, they's a-comin'!"

The crowd divided into an avenue, as before a wedding-party. And certainly no bride ever looked more modest or more radiantly happy than Miss Rachel as she came through the black old doorway into the sunset light. Her head was lifted now, looking the world in the face.

"Mrs. Overton," she said, turning to the group behind her, "this is Mr. Richard Redford, my relation from America."

"Very pleased, I'm sure," said Mrs. Overton.

"Very pleased, I'm sure," said Mr. Overton, the chief "gaffer" at the Nelson Works; to maintain the prosperity of which he came to church once a month; for, as he said, if you don't go too often they think more of you when you do.

"I was going to ask," Miss Rachel continued, "if you would show Mr. Redford the short path to the Anchor; it's on your way to the Rock Houses. He will return to my cottage for supper."

She had practised her part over during the sermon.

"Very pleased, I'm sure," was the double answer.

The daughter Madge said nothing, but stood

by, very slender and demure. Her hair was one of the scandals of the village, and to-night she felt that it was more outrageous than ever in its wild and brown profusion. Solemn elms stood in lines around the churchyard, and night already hung in their branches. As she looked up at them, a mystery as of night came into her eyes, and all the way home her heart was full of shy wonderment.

Miss Rachel watched them out of sight, and as she turned towards her cottage, two or three of her acquaintance closed on her, thirsty for biography and applied ethics.

Fetching a wide compass as became a young widow and a diplomatist, Mrs. Greaves began: "Why, Miss Rachel, I thought you'd given up the church and taken to using the chapel."

"Only when the paths are dirty."

"That all? And I've been and told the rector's wife you'd become a sectary because of that pillow-case of the rector's you put new buttons on as it was going up from the wash, because you'd caught sight of the brass rims working their way through the covers!"

"I bear no malice," said Miss Rachel.

"And what's more, I told her of that thing

you said—how you wouldn't have minded for a Nonconformist, but you did like to see the Church kept decent. She wasn't best pleased with that."

"There was no need to repeat it," said Miss Rachel.

"Decent, indeed!" continued the widow, with fermenting wrath. "A parson is a man, I suppose, and decent and a man are two things that don't go together, my dear. But of course you know nothing about that—not so far."

"I never had a brother," said Miss Rachel.

Her friends looked at each other sideways.

"You know nothing, my dear, or else you'd be blushing the other side of your face. The brass coming through the buttons isn't the only thing that makes you wish yourself dead, as soon as you start keeping a man in the house. I can speak free, having buried mine. But you'll stand to what I say, Mrs. Upcott?"

"Mrs. Greaves," was the oracular reply, "a man in the house is worth two pigs in a poke."

"And then there's the labour to feed and wash him."

"Mrs. Greaves, a woman's life is first catch your man, then cook for him."

"And the treatment he gives you in return for his meals!"

"Mrs. Greaves, it's killing the goose to make sauce for the gander."

"O Miss Rachel, to think what you've been spared!"

"Well, I don't know. It must be nice to make any one happy," said Miss Rachel.

"Ay, that's right," said the tottering old grandmother, silent hitherto. "That's what my poor husband had used to say. Poor old man, I remember him well! 'Lucy,' he'd say, 'thee's done very well by me. I'll miss thee when thee's gone. I'll have to take the cat and put her against my back to keep me warm.' But 'twas him as went the first, and it's me as takes the cat. Her keeps me joost as warm; but I miss him dreadful at times, all the same."

"Your relation can't be your nephew if you hadn't a brother," suggested Mrs. Greaves. "But I suppose he's a good bit younger than you?"

"Twenty years and seven months," said Miss Rachel, with a little sigh.

"That's exact. You can tell him from me

that he isn't bad-looking—though perhaps he knows it already. Nobody would think he was of the same family as you, Miss Rachel."

"Not of the same family!" said Miss Rachel, flushing up suddenly. "Why not?"

"It isn't for me to say why not; all I say is the young man's not bad-looking. I suppose he's married?"

"Married? No! Of course he's not married."

"Well, you can tell him he's as fine-built a young man as ever I saw. I've a good mind to marry him myself."

"You never shall!" cried Miss Rachel.

"Oh, keep your temper! I could if I liked, I suppose," said the widow. "He's got the devil in his eye."

"He hasn't!" said Miss Rachel.

"And what do you know about the devil, I'd like to ask—an old maid like you?"

"I'm not an old maid—I mean, not so very old. You see, Mrs. Greaves," Miss Rachel went on more calmly, "before the boy went to America I saw him nearly every day, and knew what he did and what he thought about, and there was nothing of the devil in him at all. Besides, being my relation, he's in a sort of way bone of my bone."

"The nearer the bone, the sweeter the child," quoth Mrs. Upcott.

"His mother must be a happy woman," murmured the old lady.

"Won't you take my arm a bit, granny?" said Miss Rachel.

"It's nice to have children so long as they's little," said the old lady.

"Little and good," said the proverbial philosopher.

"I'm not denying it," said the widow. "All I say is, he's not a baby any longer. He's a fine young fellow, and a wife might be as proud of him as a mother."

"A mother's best," said the old lady. "He can't never get out of that. You may be dead and buried, but he can't never get out of you being his mother, not if he was married twenty times he can't."

"Thank God, no," said Miss Rachel.

"Ay, my dear, it would be a blessed thing to be a mother of a man like that, no matter for how."

"Yes, it *is* a blessed, blessed thing," cried Miss Rachel.

Her holy little face was like a red-hot fire, and the flames were in her eyes.

All had stopped dead, and were looking at her.

"Lord love thee, dear," said the old lady. "I knowed it all along, from the first moment I see you come in at the church door, and I says to myself, 'So that's 'cause why her took mercy on Cissy Wilson's misfortune.'"

Without another word Miss Rachel and her neighbour went on together down the field alone.

"Well, I *am* sure!" said the young widow, gulping down her heart to its former position in her bosom, and holding it there. "So that's what comes of eating seeds and creases instead of honest butcher's meat. Give me joints and roots."

"Mrs. Greaves," came the solemn answer, "I have always said, it is not the Miss that makes the maid."

When the stranger came back from the inn, Miss Rachel met him in the passage, and took his hairy hands in hers.

MISS RACHEL

"Richard," she said very quietly, "I've betrayed you. Everybody knows. I couldn't help it. I was so proud of you. I am ever so much happier than any of them, and I couldn't help telling them. It seems to burst out of me. Now you must go away again."

"No," he said; "I've decided to stop. I'm going to make this old place whirl."

"I couldn't help it," she repeated. "I am so proud. It seems to burst out of me."

"O mother," he said, "what does that matter? Do you know Madge Overton? Isn't she a wonder to see?"

X

THE TRAGEDY OF KINESTEAD

I

OLD George Overton had grown up on the Nelson Works beside the Kinestead Canal, and they were his world. Life without them was unimaginable as the life in Saturn, and his service in their cause was his sufficient reason for existence. For he was enamoured of them, as an Athenian was enamoured of Athens; and his heart rose and fell with their fortunes, as a lover's with the health or mood of his mistress. But being an English lover, he kept his feelings guarded with all the art of manly self-defence, and few could have divined the fire of devotion which glowed under his open waistcoat, and those heavy corduroy trousers which reached high above the middle ribs, and were fitted with pockets like the portholes of an ancient three-decker.

THE TRAGEDY OF KINESTEAD

But for more than a year past his confidence had been slowly eaten into by the tooth of privy care. Since the old partners died, and their sons had become impassioned, the one for drink, the other for golf, things had never been quite the same at the Works. For a few months no definite evidence could be named, but the intuitive perception of love was harassed by vague uncertainty, and old George lived and moved uneasy as a dog in a house where ghosts begin to walk. Workmen know little of causes —as little as a private soldier knows of a campaign; and true workmen seldom speak of what they know. But it was rumoured that orders were falling off; that smaller works were turning out as good a quality of iron cheaper; that the famous Trafalgar stamp of "best best cable" was being forged, and nothing said. One afternoon the golfing partner, exhilarated to gambling pitch by a round on the Malvern links, had a bright vision of steel. Fresh capital was raised, and steel plant erected. The costly sheds with their gay crimson roofs now stood ready. Steel was to be made; but, as old George said, "it dallied"—and dallied was the right word for the flimsy, flashy, fashionable thing, so different from the trusty iron of good old days. His life was sapped with forebodings. He could only hope that if nothing else happened, the Works might still pull through. To pull through somehow is the English art.

Then arrived this bearded young engineer, with a big hat—"Miss Rachel's babby," as he was called; and certainly he made things "whirl." From the north of England, where he was bred as a boy, he brought all manner of new methods of working the coal, and in Pittsburg he had learnt something about iron. Going straight up to the partners, as if there was not a pin to choose between them and a puddler at the furnace, he carried the old Works by storm. The drinking partner feared and avoided him; but the golfer trusted him more and more, and kept him always at his elbow—except, of course, upon the links. The men liked him well enough for his good-humoured indifference to all their chaff about his parentage. Even old George said he had seen bigger fools. For Richard could respect iron, though as yet he had not penetrated to its shy and secret depths. Where iron was concerned, no trouble seemed too much for him. He would sit up all a night-shift through, after the long day's work, to watch some new process of growth in that stern child of earth and fire. And now for weeks past he had been scheming and labouring upon a wonderful new machine which was to rejuvenate the whole system of puddling—an unromantic name for so delicate a function.

"You'd best leave it alone," growled old George. "Iron's a livin' thing, and you never know when she mayn't bring you up with a smack in the mouth if you keep on meddlin' and doin'. You can't play none of your Yankee tricks with iron, no more than with a female."

Richard laughed, but did not take his eyes off the furnace which he was watching with half-closed lids. The cinder had stopped boiling over in gleaming jets through the mouth, and now the iron itself was rising through the cinder to the top. In the midst of the dazzling brilliance of heat, the iron grain, like little bubbles of fire, could just be distinguished leaping and scurrying about. Two naked puddlers with long rabbles and paddles kept working and stirring at the flux through the narrow portal of the furnace. With the fine touch of habit they were slowly moulding the ore into five great "balls," or masses ready for the hammer. Now and again they drew out their rods, white-hot for half their length, and plunged them hissing into a long water-trough.

"You'd best leave it alone, yoong mairster," old George went on, after watching the men at their work with the proud but critical air of a schoolmaster whose boy has at last composed a decent elegiac couplet. "Forty year I've stood by these furnaces watchin' and workin' for the best choice of stooff to mix and marry, the fat and the lean together. And when you've got 'em layin' comfortable in the furnace, do you think iron's the kind of thing to stand a machine interferin' with it? You might as well get married by machinery yerself."

"Well, what's the parson for, anyhow?" said Richard, with his cheery laugh.

But old George moved sadly away. "All I'm sayin'," he muttered, "is as you can't do nothing with iron unless you mix brains to it and treat it lovin', seein' as it's a livin' creatur'."

He started on his usual rounds through the sheds, watching the familiar scene of cheerful activity. At some of the furnaces the "heat" was already finished, and the great balls, glowing like the sun, were being drawn out and rolled away on trolleys to the shinglers, who stood, cased in aprons and masks, waiting to seize them with tongs and thrust them under the helves. Down swung those giant hammers, crushing them into soft shapes like bricks for a palace in hell, whilst on every side the cinder flakes were shed. Beaten into form, the oblong masses were run off to the rollers, and passed to and fro through the narrowing grooves, till they looked no thicker than fiery serpents, pliant and sparkling from head to tail. Dragged to the measuring place, they were cut into lengths by the shrieking saw, stamped with the brand, and at last, still showing a clouded red with now and then a spurt of flame, were laid side by side, till fire and man should again soften and divide and weld them to be the trust of iron navies. Certainly iron was a living thing, not to be tampered with. It was to old George what the British Constitution was to Burke. His forebodings increased his love, and under the top of his trousers his heart grew heavier.

At mid-day the bull blew, and the chattering girls who had been waiting on the bridge over the steaming canal, were let in at the gates, each bearing the recognised basket and bottle, or an earthenware bowl tied up in a coloured handkerchief. Men and boys were soon scattered through the Works to their several nooks, content as gods in the enjoyment of food and the winter sunshine which sparkled from the crystals on the meadows and hills. By the side of their males sat the girls, half turned away out of feminine delicacy; for, as they knew by instinct, all animals fear to be watched at solitary meals.

The last to come was old George's daughter Madge, her eyes and face bright with speed and frosty air. A lover's dinner is no weight to carry, but still it made two, and she had to call for it at Miss Rachel's cottage on the way. As "gaffer," old George had a quiet corner of a shed to himself, cut off from the world by a rusted boiler. There she found him and Richard seated on planks beside a burning brazier. The old man said nothing, but sighed; and when he had devoured all his food with the appetite natural to melancholy, he went away without a word, rubbed a piece of paper against a cooling bar, lighted his pipe with it, and turned to solitude to eat his heart.

"Richard," said Madge, watching the thin blue flames in the brazier, with her hands clasped round her knees, "what are these Iron Men that everybody's talking about?"

"That's my invention. I've thought of nothing else day and night for weeks."

"It's to save the puddlers, isn't it?" she asked.

"No, it's to save expense."

"Father's quiet and close, but he isn't a fool," she went on after a pause. "Richard, you'd do best to give up this invention."

"Give up the Iron Men? Never."

"For my sake!"

"For no man or woman on earth."

"But I love you. For you I could give up everything."

"The Iron Men will be at work to-night."

He sat on the ground at her feet, and put his head between her knees, whilst she passed her fingers through his hair and stroked his face, bending gravely over him. The whirl and clatter of the Works sounded around them, but the old boiler gave them a sanctuary.

"How proud every one is of you," she said. "It is so sweet to hear them talk."

"Are you proud of me too?"

"I proud of you? No. I love you. You are everything to me."

"Not everything yet. What shall I be soon?"

"Dearest of men you always are."

"What else?"

"You know what else."

"Say it, then—say it," he urged.

"No, I dare not say it. We must not be too happy."

The noise of the Works seemed so far away that the bottom of the motionless sea is not more silent than was that little corner of the clanging shed.

When the winter evening fell, and the night-shift came to work, the Iron Men stood ready in position before two of the puddling furnaces. All hands gathered round the scene, their faces turned to orange under the glow of fire. As they watched, the heavy iron bars along the roof began to move, and the two rods suspended from them in front of the furnace mouths advanced and retired with almost mysterious solemnity, like ghosts on duty.

To a pivot hinge at the end of one Richard hooked a long rabble, and worked it to and fro into every corner of the furnace with one hand like a child's toy. Deep oaths revealed the astonished enthusiasm of the crowd. The golfing partner clapped Richard on the back, and in all his life never came so near to making a speech. The day-shift departed, but all night long the puddlers remained, excited, and emulous to be instructed in the new machines. Never was such a happy night known in the Works. In the early morning Richard was conducted home with songs and shouting under stars which were pale as the frozen snow beneath them on the hills. At the garden gate some one called for cheers for Miss Rachel's babby. Richard took off his cap, and wondered if Madge heard them in her rock-cut chamber farther down the valley. He turned, and felt his mother's arms around him, trembling for joy.

But all that night old George had stood amazed between the furnaces. He was like a blind old king who in the midst of the castle's revelry hears an unknown fate knocking at the wintry door.

II

The next scene fell in midsummer weather; but in the meantime fate had knocked and entered—the Nelson Works, like Troy, were in the past.

Two days after Richard's triumph the partners had announced that owing to the labour-saving machinery newly erected at great cost, only half the number of puddlers would be required. The remainder were thoughtfully advised to look for other employment. Their names were read out, and, as they heard their doom, the more demonstrative among them muttered, "That's a oner!" or simply, "O Christ!"

In the evening old George presided over a solemn council at the Anchor. Weighty with piety, he took his seat on a Windsor chair half consecrated by age. He briefly stated the situation, and called attention for the speakers.

Two spoke, repeating what old George had said. Then he himself summed up, repeating what he had said at the beginning. He put the question. Every one knew old George, the man he was. Every one was of his opinion. He finished off his beer, and went home to bed without a word, knowing that his life was over.

Next morning the puddlers stood in a body upon the bridge over the steaming canal, and watched it cool. Sometimes they varied their inaction by spitting into it.

Old George listened to the furnaces ticking and cracking as they slowly died out. The Iron Men moved idly backwards and forwards in front of them without pause. Any one who wished to express emotion cursed them and their maker.

On the morrow the Works stood deserted, and the canal was frozen over. Wild rumours flew. With the vague terrors of the poor, men looked round before they spoke their minds. It was said the partners were meeting the investors, that capital shook like jelly, melted away like a snail, was become barren paper, no more yielding the double crop of comfortable gold. Causes were conjectured —the drink, a mortal thing in skirts near Birmingham; but all agreed it was really the Iron Men who with iron hands were taking the bread from warm mouths of flesh and blood. Had the masters, then, no hearts? It was known they had. The young golfer was a man beloved. He would see justice done.

Under the frosty moon a white placard appeared upon the gates. A fortnight's work with extra pay was offered to all hands, to complete a contract. The Works would then be permanently closed.

Through that fortnight old George went about like a man whose wife lies unburied and does not yet seem wholly gone. The final evening came, and the old bull roared and screamed. No poetic swan-song bidding farewell was ever yet so sad. In silence the men rose up, and drew on their dingy coats. Collecting their blackened cans, and giving one look round for other bits of things, they huddled through the trampled snow out of the old black gates, which shut clanging behind them.

By a happy economic law, labour, when

THE TRAGEDY OF KINESTEAD 203

there is no longer a demand for it in a particular locality, tends to adjust itself like water, the workmen becoming absorbed in other lucrative occupations.

So day after day the Kinestead workmen stood on the canal bridge, and stared at the familiar Works.

The first to be absorbed was the millwright, Joseph Beals. After prolonged thrift he had begun to erect a pretty cottage for his family. There was nothing now for him to save off; so he went mad, and was absorbed in the County Lunatic Asylum.

A few old men, missing their accustomed exercise, and having time for the consideration of their health, were absorbed in the churchyard.

A few others, demoralised by uncertainty and want of work, were absorbed in the public-house.

The remainder went twice a day up to the bridge, and stared at the desolate Works.

Everybody said the Works were sure to reopen, next week perhaps, or next month. The great Marquis was going to buy them up. He was a true sportsman, and ran straight on the turf. He was giving up a horse and a woman to save the village. A young man went over the Works taking notes. Old George showed him round, and no doubt he was agent for the Marquis. But the young man turned an honest five shillings by making a paragraph out of the disaster for a local newspaper, and sent a copy of it with compliments and thanks. Old George framed it neatly in a funeral card, and nailed it up on his wall.

Hunger laid its hand upon the village, and women began to sell the rind of possessions which forms around and shelters each core of life—clocks and cloths and ornaments and tables, such as neighbours might decently be asked to purchase. There was a panic of sale. Why leave anything a landlord might seize for a payment so barren as rent? It was exciting and sportsman-like to elude him, and point only to bare walls and a bed.

Then was organised that Kinestead Relief Fund for which the hollow-cheeked collectors visited Wenley with their soiled little account-books and their tale of all the woe. They tramped far out into the unknown country, to the great river and the southern plain, where men still tended flocks and ploughed the patient earth. Even the hard bowels of the husbandmen could not refuse a penny. The golfing partner subscribed fifty pounds, the parson a sovereign. A torch-light procession of weary forms, each shaped by long use to his separate piece of work, brought in something. Every Friday old George distributed the Fund in cash and groceries, and it was received with hang-dog sullenness more pathetic than all the tears and groans of literature.

In summer the sale of the plant in the Works began, and was watched day by day, as piece by piece the machinery and even the iron roofs were lifted into deep barges, and glided out of sight. When the Iron Men were broken up and stacked, their fall was greeted by laughter and angry cheers. But the turn of the rollers came next, and on one of them Jem Bartlet, a big shingler, was found quietly seated. "Beg pardon, gen'lemen," he said, "but this 'ere roller's the one as my boy James was passed through." The night was well remembered when the boy's leg had been caught between the roller's lips, and he was sucked screaming through them, to emerge in unspeakable bars on the other side. That roller was left with the father sitting upon it.

Next day the great fly-wheel was loaded up, and vanished like the rest. An unwilling groan arose from the people as it went. It was the heart of the Works, and now that it was gone the Nelson Works were indeed dead for ever, and there was no hope left for rumour to build on.

When old George came home that evening he only said, "The fly-wheel's gone." His wife cried over the table, and Madge curled herself between his knees.

There was no more to be said. He had still enough laid by to save him from coming on the Fund, and he really had been absorbed into "another lucrative occupation," having been appointed grave-digger to the parish for his invariable integrity and occasional conformity. To distract his mind, he took up a borrowed newspaper, and read this paragraph: "We hear that the junior partner in the Nelson Works has been compelled to leave his superb mansion near Kinestead, and will reside at Malvern, where he will no doubt find some consolation in the royal game of golf, to which he is so passionately devoted. This only establishes our contention that the interests of capital and labour are identical, and rise or fall together in true solidarity."

"Poor boy! oh, poor boy!" murmured old George, and for the first time on record his eyes filled with tears. "He's got to coom down to a smaller 'ouse, and it's all along of them Iron Men and him who made them."

Madge drew her shoulders together, but she waited till he assumed the shamefaced look of an Englishman detected in a display of grief. Then she passed out into the summer evening, and up the village street, where the dreary unemployed just raised their heads to look after her. She chose a narrow path across the common at the foot of Kinestead Beacon, and entered woods of birch and pine. The bracken had uncurled its opening hand. Now and again a tree rustled and swayed under a squirrel's leap.

As her lover drew near, she marked his haggard look and stooping walk. Care and disappointment were having their way with him. The sleepless snakes of idleness and uncertainty were gnawing at his strength. Man has other plagues—ill-health, jealousy, religious doubts, and death. The man who is out of work justly makes light of them all. According to most forms of religion, a corpse is in more hopeful case than he.

"Richard," she said at once, "you must go from this place. I've come to say good-bye."

"Everybody has turned against me, so you drive me away?" he answered.

She took his hand and laid it across her mouth, undoing the clenched fingers one by one.

"Will you come with me, then?" he asked.

"No. We must say good-bye. I could never leave my own people in distress—never. What happiness could we two have together now? You can buy happiness too dear. Somebody has to pay."

The man's strength was already broken. He sunk into a bitter stupor, and few more words were said.

"Say good-bye to me just once more," she pleaded. "You won't? Then good-bye, good-bye, dear love, for ever."

She kissed his shoulder, and when the squirrel peeped round the white stem of a birch he saw that she was alone and reassuringly still.

"Mother," said Richard, when he got home, "you can keep the rest of the money I made in America. I'm going back again now."

"Yes, dear," said Miss Rachel, turning white; "it's best for you to go."

"Do me up something to eat, and I'll catch this next train. It'll be grand to get away."

"Yes, Richard, grand!" said Miss Rachel, and went into her clean and fragrant larder.

Just at sunset Richard started for the station by the path across the fields. Having nothing further to hope for, he had ceased to despair; and there was an angry satisfaction in cutting himself free from the past, and letting the future do its worst. All the joyless but real compensations of a thwarted lover were his as he looked at the ruined Works and the familiar valley in the service of which he had laboured. For the natural man feels a natural consolation in the knowledge that the blow which pierces his heart goes also to the heart of his lost mistress.

As he glanced savagely round, Richard saw some one sitting on the third stile, but he paid no attention to him till he came near and found him to be Patsy Connor, apparently waiting for anything that might happen next in this muddle of a world. Patsy had been one of the labourers in the Works, and nature made him inevitably a favourite. No misfortune had been able to sour or depress his spirit. He was living quite happily upon the Relief Fund, and intended to continue living on it as long as it lasted. But against Richard he bore a very private grudge; for he could love each woman in the world to distraction, and he made it a rule to love the nearest best; but he could not endure to imagine any feminine being accepting and returning any man's love except his own. Without moving from the stile, therefore, he cried: "Hullo! Here comes Miss Rachel's barstard, skulkin' off."

"Come, none of that, Patsy," said Richard, laying a hand on his shoulder. "Let's pass, or it may be the worse for you."

"Oh, it'll be the worse for me, will ut?" cried Patsy, springing up, whilst the quick blood rushed through his brain. "And I'd like to know where you've left my sweet girl Madge that you've been tryin' to make the same sort of thing of, as your mother was afore you!"

The two men stood facing each other, their

eyes bright with the longing for hard and open conflict after all those months of slackness and dreary waiting. They seemed to stand there a very long time. Richard noticed the red handkerchief tied in a lover's knot round Patsy's neck, and the swollen blue veins above it. A smell of meadow-sweet came from the ditch beside the hedge, and in the silence he heard a late lark singing as it hovered down the sky. He dropped his bundle, and as at a signal they sprang upon each other with a sigh of pleasure, and closed, struggling fiercely up and down the path. Within the first minute Patsy slipped in some half-dried mud, and they fell, but shook themselves free, and rose panting and glaring at each other with a shamefaced look from which the joy was gone.

"Look here, Patsy," said Richard, "you never mean what you say. If you've had enough to keep your tongue quiet, I'll go on."

"Well, you see, it's for a woman," said Patsy, hesitating, for they had always been good friends at the Works.

"Oh, if you meant it, all right," said Richard, and they rushed at each other again. But before they met, Richard struck one great blow home on the side of the head, and Patsy fell groaning. When he rose he held in his right hand a short keen-edged knife with a black handle. To both of them it now seemed quite natural that it should be so, and they walked round each other at three paces distance, watching for the chance. Patsy gave a quick pull at his coat sleeve to clear his wrist, and somehow the movement suggested to Richard a small alteration in the construction of his Iron Men. The lark was still singing, but in a feeble fluttering voice, being near its plunge for home. It stopped, and Patsy sprang. Richard caught the hand which grasped the knife, and held it above their heads by the wrist. Again they closed and struggled together. Each knew that this time it was for life and all. Their faces touched each other, cheek to cheek, like lovers, and were moist with each other's sweat. They trampled far over the grass deep with flowers, the knife still raised high above them. A solitary cow came and looked at them, and made a pretence to butt, and gambolled awkwardly away. Suddenly Richard found his leg coiled behind Patsy's, and he felt they were again falling together. Dragging the knife downwards, he forced its point against Patsy's side. It took an extraordinarily long time for them to fall, and he carefully avoided letting Patsy drop into a heap of dirt upon the grass. At last they touched ground, and Richard's whole weight fell on the two hands which held the knife. The point seemed to stop against something hard, and then it went quietly on its way, down, down, as softly as into butter.

Richard started up, and helped Patsy to his feet. Each stared at the other in amazement, and laughed nonsensically, like two lunatics meeting on a walk for exercise. Patsy looked all round the sky, and then very slowly turned his eyes down towards the hand which was still pressed against his side. It was all wet and red. "Oh, oh, oh!" he cried, and would have fallen, but Richard held him up and guided him to the stile.

"Why, what's the matter, Patsy? You're surely not hurt—not to speak of?"

"Then look at me poor blood runnin' out," said Patsy, and leaned backwards against the stile.

"Fetch a doctor, quick, my dear, afore it spoils me shirt and weskit."

He slid down upon the earth, and gazed with appealing eyes up at Richard, who was leaning over him.

"Be Jasus," he murmured, as his face turned yellow, "poor dear Patsy's goin' to die. Beg pardon, sure; it was my fault most entirely."

His head swung off the post to one side, disturbing the leisurely progress of a fat beetle with purple legs, which with an obstinate sense of direction proceeded to crawl arduously over his face. Richard watched it till it reached the bloodless mouth, and then dashed it hurriedly away with his hand. He looked round and saw that the evening had suddenly grown dark. The train was waiting in the station, and they were putting lighted lamps into the carriages. People were coming in haste across the fields, perhaps afraid of being late for it. He recognised a woman's voice, and the chemist's. A causeless but irresistible fear came over him. He crept through the stile, and ran for his life, keeping under the shelter of the hedge. He remembered he had left his bundle behind. He thought of going back for it, and making explanations; but the irresistible power drove him on, and each step made return impossible.

III

He ran for a long way, and then he suddenly remembered it would be safer not to run. He found himself on the edge of a wood, and creeping under the brambles of the ditch, he lay still for a very long time and listened. A hen chaffinch was making comfortable little noises to her fledgelings in her nest of hair and lichen above his head. The summer wind sighed through the trees. A labourer shuffled along the road, singing with beery voice. Richard had lost the power of thought. He could not control the convulsive shudders which passed over his body and made the brambles rustle. His one idea was to keep rubbing his hands with leaves or tufts of grass. Unexpectedly the old Kinestead church on the opposite hill struck eleven. He raised his head and peered along the field through the stalks of daisies and sorrel. There was a lantern at the very gate, and some one was climbing over. He crept through a gap into the wood, and stole from tree to tree, till a narrow path led him down a steep bank to the canal. He heard a shout behind him, and another answering it. Hurrying along the tow-path, he came to the Rock Houses, cut like caves years ago in the face of the red sandstone cliff. He could not have said why he came there; he did not know he had thought of Madge at all since that thing had happened by the stile. But only the Overtons lived in the houses now, and their rooms had been cut up and down the cliff wherever opportunity afforded, and were connected by narrow galleries and steps inside.

Below one of the windows, which was about twelve feet above the path, Richard stopped and listened again. He heard another shout, but it seemed more distant. He longed to speak to some human creature, and tell how the thing had really happened. As he looked back on the distant afternoon, and thought of Madge and her face as she said good-bye, a passionate desire for love and pity came over him. Scrambling up the few feet of rock, he laid his hands upon the window-sill. The window was wide open, and the night air passed in and out where Madge lay sleeping on a pillow wet with tears.

At the first sound she sprang from her bed, and stood white from head to foot in the glimmer which is always either lingering or approaching through a summer night.

"Oh, dearest love, is it you?" she whispered, putting her hands on his. "Oh, I thought I should never see you again!"

Silently he dragged himself up, and swung into the room. "Quick!" he said; "they are hunting me. They are close behind. Where can I hide?"

"Hide in my heart, beloved. No one will dare to find you there."

She caught him to her breast, and clung to him so that he might not see her.

"Oh, you mustn't touch me," he groaned; "I am covered with blood."

"I thought I should never see you again, dear love, and now you have come. Oh, is it really you? How sweet you are to forgive me! How could I live without you? I never meant a word of what I said."

"I have killed a man," he said dreamily, looking round the tiny chamber in the rock.

"Oh, what does anything matter if I have you?" she answered, understanding only her joy.

"It was Patsy Connor, the man they called

the Uncrowned King, because he was so happy. We fought, and I've killed him."

"Oh, not Patsy, Richard! Why, Patsy loved me. He was like a little child."

"Hush!" he whispered, suddenly tightening his arms round her. Neither of them breathed nor stirred. Footsteps were coming softly along the dusty path. They heard low voices. A light flashed across the red stone ceiling. It came again—a round disc of light.

"What's that winder doin' open?" murmured a man's voice below.

"It's always open of a summer," said another. "That's where Madge Overton goes to bed. I once climbed up this tree to take a look at 'er."

They were the two guardians of Kinestead's innocence.

"Madge Overton?" said the other. "Why, it's her I've been thinking of all along. Seems to me she's most likely at the bottom of all this business. That fellow's been keepin' company with her for months past. And as to Patsy—well, we all know Patsy, the kind of fellow he is with the girls. I'll lay she knows more than most of us. You stand by with the lantern and I'll just take a look in at that window."

"You'd best not. You can't never know what a girl like her mightn't do at you afore you got up. If I was you, I'd be afraid of gettin' hurt."

"Give us a back up," said the other, and the scraping of an ironed boot was heard upon the rock. Very softly Madge pushed her lover back into a corner by the door, drew a hanging dress over him, and slid under the sheet on her bed.

"Now shine the lantern as high as you can," whispered a hoarse voice close below the window. The disc of light reappeared, and the man's deep breathing sounded very loud as he struggled to pull his weight up on to the sill. Madge turned on her bed and threw out an arm, moaning as if in dreams.

"Is that you, father?" she murmured. Then sitting up in bed, she cried, "Who's there?" and sprang to the window, above the edge of which the policeman's head was just visible. Her white night-gown was so close to his eyes he could see nothing else in the room.

"Beg pardon for disturbing you, Missie," he said, "but we're the police looking for somebody, and we thought he might be somewhere hereabouts."

"How dare you think any one could be here? Get down, or I'll call for my father!"

"No offence, Missie, but you see it's that Richard Redford of yours we're looking for. He's gone and done something bad."

"What's he done? He's gone away by the train. I told him to go. I hate him."

"Oh, well, of course if you hate him, that's a different story, and it's no good me trying to cling on here any more. Only I thought you'd like to know he'd stabbed Patsy Connor, and for all I know, Patsy's now laying in the hospital ready to be screwed down—more's the pity."

"Not Patsy! Oh, don't say Patsy!" she cried, and fell forward upon the sill, covering her face with her arms.

Unable to retain his hold any longer, the policeman dropped to the ground with a heavy thud.

"You see, I was right," he whispered to his companion. "We're on the track now. That's what they call detecting the motive. I knew it 'ud be a woman. Poor thing! look at her how she lays there and takes on."

THE TRAGEDY OF KINESTEAD 221

"Well," replied the other reflectively, " I never did hold much with barstards. Now I come to think of it, I can't say I ever did. But I'm for getting back to the gas-lamps. You never know what a man like that mightn't do at you, jumping out in the dark. We'll catch him right enough by daylight."

"Oh yes, we'll catch him. We've got at his motive now, and any judge will tell you that's the first thing. So, good-night, Missie, and I'm sorry for you from my heart."

When the last sound of their footsteps had died away, Madge drew a long breath, and passed her hand wearily over her forehead. Her lover was by her side. She felt that his body was still trembling with convulsive shudders.

"Dear love, you are cold," she said, and nestled close to him, laying her hot cheek against his.

"Oh, Madge," he moaned, "I can hear nothing but Patsy crying out. He looked at his hand and cried out."

"Forget it now, dear; we must only think of what to do next."

"My hand was red too."

"See, then, I put it close against my heart

to warm. Oh, do not shudder so. Do you not love me? We must think now, and wait here till all the world is quiet outside."

She sorted out her oldest clothes, and dressed hurriedly. Then they waited side by side, the pulse of her blood measuring out the passing minutes. Richard spoke no more, but with his head on her breast he moaned restlessly, like a dream-haunted child. Suddenly the first grey light of a summer morning came upon them with surprise, and found them still seated on the edge of a wooden box, cold and pale as ghosts. Madge stole to the window. Outside a thick white mist clung to the ground along the valley, and above it rose the heavy elms still black with night. But the sky overhead was already hollow and deep, and only the largest stars could now be seen. There was a sound of multitudes of larks, leaping up to divide the night from day. The cattle, hidden by the mist, sighed contentedly in the flat meadow across the canal.

"Beloved!" she whispered, "I have thought what to do. Quick, and help me down. Do you think I could stay apart from you now?"

Like a man in a trance, Richard let himself

down the face of the rock again. She clung for a moment to the window and dropped silently into his arms. Through grass and sleeping flowers they crept noiselessly to the edge of the canal. There the mist covered them as safely as a white sheet, and they sped away, silent and unseen, through the invisible land. In turn the different birds awoke and called, and little by little the mist grew thinner, till above them they could almost see the sky; but the human world was still asleep. In the corner of a field they stopped, and Madge rubbed her face with earth, tore her skirt into a fringe, dipped it in the canal, and trailed it through the dust. Then with scissors she cut her lover's beard close to the skin. "Now make your face and clothes like mine," she whispered, as though afraid of being overheard, "and we'll do."

They sat down under a whitewashed bridge and waited. Just as the sun was rising, a barge-horse, driven by a boy, came straining along on its toes, and the painted bows of a monkey-boat pushed through the mist. Waiting till it reached the narrows of the bridge, Madge started up and cried to the man at the tiller: "Hi, mairster! give we a bit of a lift, there's a darlin'! My poor mon's fair clemmed, and can't slother along for another step. Do 'e now, and I'll take it kind, and make it kind."

The bargeman looked her sleepily down from head to foot, and she smiled her sweetest.

"Joomp in, if yer can," he said, swinging the rudder till the stern almost grazed the bricks. The barge was heavy, being laden with refuse from the Nelson Works; and the Iron Men were on board among the rest.

Madge and Richard crept into the little cabin, painted with a castle embowered in roses, and lay down side by side on the floor at the bargeman's feet. Soon the sun beat hot upon the wooden roof, and all day long the barge drove its slow course through silent waters between the sunny fields. About once an hour the bargeman stooped to look at the sleeping tramps. "Blime!" he said each time, and went on with his steering. When the barge tied up for the night, he woke them. Just as she leapt ashore, the girl laid her hand softly upon his mouth. "Blime! Well, I never did!" he said, as they disappeared in the darkness.

And now the Nelson Works are only to be

traced by lines of foundations half hidden under French willow and loosestrife. The Rock Houses are deserted, and in the sandstone roof of Madge's chamber the mason bee has built her nest, and hums around the door of her burrow.

.

XI

GEORDIE'S MARROW

It was just six o'clock on a bitter winter's morning at Wenley-on-the-Hill. The sky was still covered with night, but starless; and the earth seemed to throw up against it a pale reflection from her own deep snows. The smooth white roofs of the village, showing clear above the invisible walls, gave the houses a look of children's toys. Dark as it was, a few dark figures could be seen slowly stealing up the snowy street, on which there was as yet no track of wheels or footprints. They were the cold and sleepy miners on their way to the pits for day-shift. Under the gaunt and gallows-like stack at the mouth of the Trigger Pit, Shadow was trampling the snow impatiently, and trying to fan a warmth in his bosom by whistling "The Campbells are Coming" as a pibroch, with long intervals of groaning accompaniment. All the time he kept a general's look-out for the mustering of his forces. It was the custom for all hands to go down the pit by half-past six, even though they knew they would be at once sent up again to "play," because orders were slack. This was thought a salutary discipline for the spirit, like the eight o'clock services in the warmed and lighted chapels of the universities.

As usual, the first to appear at the stack was a powerful, clean-shaven collier with a surly or taciturn manner and a strange look of defiance in his eyes. He was a pikeman from the North—a hewer, he called himself—and as he came from Durham, of course his name was Geordie. Close behind him trudged a queer slip of a boy, his inseparable companion—his "marrow," as the miners had learnt to call him, slightly perverting the strict use of the Northern word. For by "marrow" they simply meant partner, or "half-stent," as they themselves would have said. The boy was tallish and very slim. He had his hair cropt close, till it was brown and velvety as the back of a field-mouse. He always wore enormous boots, much too loose for him, and a bluish shirt, which it was supposed he never took off. Certainly he had no need to strip down in the pit like the rest, for he was only a driver as yet, and in consequence that shirt was rather to be called black than blue. Yet it harmonised well with his face and arms, which looked black past washing, and were as black in the morning as at night. Only once had a streak of white skin been visible through the cloud of coal-dust, and Shadow had called it the hope of Sunlight. But it never reappeared, and the boy was known as Dirty Dick.

This was the more strange because Geordie was quite indecently clean, and when he stripped did not even show the "collier's ring," or line of natural demarcation where clothes leave off and washing begins, but, like those superior people in the North, he washed all over every day. He practised other nasty Northern customs as well—sat on his heels to pick, rather preferred the narrow workings, and was indifferent to pigeons. The Butty only kept him because he was short of hands for a contract, and found that Geordie could send up sixteen tubs to any other pikeman's fifteen. Besides, he never drank, and always volunteered for remote or dangerous workings, where he would be likely to be posted alone with his "marrow." When the day-shift came up at four o'clock, they were always the last, and they went straight home to their cottage at the top of the hill. They kept house for themselves, and late at night Dick came out to shop, still black as sin. Through the chinks in the blind it could be seen that they had very little furniture. The bed was placed right opposite the street door, as is the Northern custom, and the door was always kept shut and bolted. Well, if they did not wish to be sociable, no one could object. An Englishman's house is his prison, locked on the inside.

"Hullo, Zulu!" said Shadow, swinging his safety-lamp in the boy's face. "What soap's that you're advertisin' this mornin'?"

"Same as your old woman washes the blood off yer carvin' sword with," retorted Dick, knowing Shadow's martial soul and single estate. But as he spoke he saw Geordie shiver and look behind him.

"All right, ole man," he said, as all three stepped together on to the cage. "You've got a bit of a chill on you from us workin' yesterday with the water bleedin' through out of the pound on us. We'll get old Job to stick us in a warmer place to-day."

"Steady up, Geordie," cried Shadow, as he gave the signal for the engineman to lower away. "You jolly well keep 'old on that there chain, or in 'alf a minute you'll be in a warmer place nor ever old Job can give yer."

The bands were already moving, and the wheels spun round this way and that under them, when suddenly a figure raced up out of the darkness, and seemed to be calling to the party to stop. But neither Shadow nor Dick saw it. The railings fell clattering into their place round the pit's mouth, and the figure was left staring over them at Shadow's lamp, which grew fainter and fainter as the cage rushed down, bumping now and then against the uneven brickwork of the shaft.

"You're nigh on 'alf an hour afore time, as you velly always be. There's only the Doggies down as yet," said Shadow, as they lighted their tallow dips and plastered the ends round with balls of wet clay. "You'd best get along to the black hole, seein' you've took a fancy for it. I'll tell Job, and send the Marshal after yer, afore you've got two tubs loaded. The old pit's goin' full gate to-day."

"Forward the Light Brigade!" cried Dick, and away he went along the gallery, teaching the groves of pit-props to resound the name of Annie Laurie. Geordie followed him in silence along the dusty track between the rails.

As soon as they were out of sight and hearing, Dick turned and said in a low voice, "Why, what was the matter, Geordie?"

Geordie looked up with a wild terror in his eyes, and then tramped on in silence.

"Sorry I said that about the sword," Dick continued.

"Oh, it wasn't that," said Geordie. "Didn't you see it?"

"No. See what?"

"Why, something black ran up to the pit's mouth as we started down. It looked over at me. I've never seen it so plain before."

"O Geordie, there was nothing there!"

"No; there was nothing there, of course. That's just the worst of it."

"There, Geordie, there," said Dick soothingly.

"You slept badly last night. It'll pass. In time it won't come again—in time."

"The thing has often been done before. Do you think all the others have suffered like me?"

"You mustn't think about it at all, Geordie. It's driving us mad. Of course it's been done before. It's quite common. It doesn't count. Besides we're safe now."

"O Dick, I almost wish we weren't. I wish I was caught, and all over."

"Doesn't *us* count for nothink, then?" said Dick, with a pitiful attempt at a smile on his black face, where a line of white teeth showed for a moment.

There was no answer, and they crept along the branching galleries in silence—two flames of human life, so deep below the fields and rivers. As they went on, the workings became narrower, and Geordie had to stoop low to avoid the slabs of timber across the top. Where the dips were steep, they had to wade through water and black slush. Sometimes they came to a door against which the current of air was beating with the noise of a torrent stream. As they violently pushed it open, the noise ceased, and then began again behind them. Sometimes the heat made the sweat start from their skins, and next moment an icy wind chilled them to the bone through their wet clothes.

At last they turned from one of the main air-ways down a new gallery, which was being cut for ventilation as well as for coal. This was the black hole Shadow mentioned, and it had now been carried forward for about seventy yards. Along the left side for part of the distance ran a made-up fire-rib to protect the mine from a fire which had been kindled by the friction of some ancient workings falling in, and was now always smouldering. In spite of the dam an almost imperceptible greenish smoke would sometimes curl through the crevices, and lie coiled along the top of the gallery—" clinging to the rough," as the miners say—till it could be carried off by a draught. But the air along the gallery itself was so stagnant now, that before Geordie and his marrow had gone twenty yards their candles began to burn dim, the heat was intense, and the silence in their ears almost terrible. When they reached the " face," Geordie took off his clothes and began the daily toil without a word. As soon as enough coal had fallen, they set about loading up the tubs side by side with forks and shovels, and before the second tub was full, a low rumble was heard approaching.

"That's the Marshal coming," said Dick, wiping his dripping face with his shirt-sleeve, and substituting a new layer of grime. The Marshal was one of Shadow's favourite ponies. Hearing Dick's answer to the shout of the driver who had brought him down with others for that part of the mine, he came of his own accord for a short distance along the stifling gallery. He was a tiny little creature, old, nearly blind, and covered with the glorious scars and wounds of service. In the happy days when he had roamed the fields beside his mother, he had perhaps been a bay. Now he was the colour that veterans wear when the long battle is nearly over. Meeting Dick on the way, he stopped, and breathing hard with the delight of recognition, rubbed his nose against his chest, taking the dirty shirt playfully between his lips in petition for the accustomed bit of sugar.

"Nice beast," said Dick, bringing the sugar

from his pocket, and stroking the soft curve of furry nose between the nostrils. "There's something still glad to have me here, anyhow."

He hooked the Marshal to the full tubs, and drove them away, seated on an iron step low down in front, with his legs stretched over the chains on each side the pony's body. He had to take the tubs far away to a main working, where he could hook them to a continuous rope which ran to the shaft. Then, after calling at another station, he returned with empty tubs to help Geordie with the loading. And so the work went on hour after hour: hewing, loading, and driving, in heat and sweat and bitter winds and blackness; the tubs rumbling along the galleries; the Doggies going their rounds; the naked pitmen cursing and clamouring for drink; the boys yelling bold metaphors at all objects living or inanimate. But in all the pit there was not a boy so wildly eloquent as Dirty Dick. It was an artistic pleasure to listen to him.

"Drink time" came at half-past twelve. Geordie and Dick emerged into the air-way, and throwing their jackets over their shoulders, sat huddled together upon a dusty scrap of sacking to devour the bread and dried haddock out of a knotted handkerchief.

"Sorry I was such a fool this morning," said Geordie. "I'm all right now. Fear runs out of me with the sweat, and so does remorse. I suppose it was nothing after all."

"Of course it was nothing," said Dick. "And never talk about remorse and things like that. It's no good thinking about the past. That doesn't matter. We've got our day's work to do. Have some more coffee. I've made it rather nice to-day."

"Most men have got something against them, I suppose," Geordie went on, taking no notice of consolation. "It must be common enough."

"Of course it's common," Dick answered, as cheerfully as if he said it for the first time. "A man ought to be very glad if he has only one thing against him. By the time I'm a man I'll have a lot more than one, I'm pretty sure."

"O Dick, he gave me such a look as he fell to the ground," said Geordie, shivering. "He was always so happy. Everybody liked him. You knew him, didn't you, Dick?"

"Of course I knew him," said Dick, dropping

his head wearily between his knees. "What does it all matter now?"

A small party of miners went merrily by, and there was a rapid interchange of miners' wit and compliment. When their laughter at Dick's shameless retorts had died away, Geordie said, "He doubled himself together over the place, and cried out—You know what he cried out."

"O Geordie," Dick moaned in answer, "why will you be always talking about it? Why can't you forget it like me? What does one man more or less matter? Look here, now—if his spirit covered with blood came and stood here, I'd go up to him and curse him to his face for making you unhappy."

Laying his hand hastily upon Dick's shoulder, Geordie peered round into the darkness. "Come along," he said at last, "let's get to work again. A man like me need be afraid of nothing—nothing real."

He threw off his coat, revealing the great muscles of his arms and chest. Dick rolled up his own shirt-sleeve, and laughed at the contrast. They groped their way back to the "face," their candles now showing little more than the blue of the flame.

"You'd better keep in the air-way with the pony," said Geordie. " It's getting a bit too thick up here. I'll shout when the tubs are ready. I've got to finish the stent. They shan't say I couldn't work, anyhow."

" Nor me either," said Dick.

" You won't ever leave me, Dick ? "

" Leave you ? What will you say next, I wonder ? How could I leave you now ? "

There was a pause, and then Dick drove the tubs away, kindling the Marshal's ardour with the chorus—

> "A little sup of milk, and a little bite of bread,
> A mighty lot of labour, and a blessed time in bed,
> A little bit of lovin', and a stone above your head ;
> Then, cheer up ! you'll soon be dead,
>   And it's over."

For two hours the work went on as before, and the time to "loose" was drawing near. Without moving to breathe the fresher air, Geordie was labouring to finish off his last two tubs. He had squatted down to "undergo" his last fall of coal. The dim candle glimmered at his side. His brain seemed numbed, and a dizzy sickness rendered him incapable of thought or memory. The world beyond that yard or two of coal had become blank, and he vaguely wondered whether he was feeling happier than usual. In the midst of his labour a new sensation came over him, but it seemed to be a very long time before he was really conscious of it. He then felt that he was being watched; that there was something looking at him from behind. The sensation seemed to come through his back. At last he stopped his pick and listened. There was no sound but the creeping of the coal. Not daring to look round, he went on with his work. Then something made him stop again, and again he listened. A lump of coal crunched behind him. "Dick," he cried, "is that you?"

There was no answer and no sound. Again he drove his pick into the coal, but he could not pull it out. There was certainly something present close behind him.

Very slowly he turned his head to look. He knew what he would see. There it was, standing motionless and watching him. The candle's tiny light showed that it was naked to the waist. Geordie gazed at it without moving.

"It's me," it said. "I knowed you from the first. Maybe you'll know me best by this."

It laid a finger on a short brown slit in its side.

"Think I'm afraid?" Geordie gasped, springing up so that his head struck against the low roof. Instinctively he lifted his candle too. It went out at once, and he was in utter darkness. He had just strength to fling his pick down the gallery, and he heard it fall without striking anything. Then a dizziness took hold of him. His limbs trembled, and he fell heavily beside the half-filled tub. The "damp," disturbed from its lurking-place, fell with him and lapped itself round his head in invisible coils and currents.

When Dick came back with the Marshal, he saw no light at the end of the working, and there was a peculiar smell in the stagnant air. Suddenly the pony stopped dead and stood shaking. Dick sprang from his seat and ran forward with a cry, but before he had taken three steps his candle went out. He threw it away, and groped along, stretching out his hands before his face. At last his boots struck against something soft, and he stumbled and fell upon it. He felt at it with his hands. It was a man's body naked to the waist.

"Geordie!" he screamed—"wake up; give me your arms and I'll drag you out."

The man only uttered the comfortable sigh of sleep. Dick put his hands upon the chest and face.

"It isn't Geordie!" he cried, throwing himself backwards, and violently shaking the body. "Here, you, whoever you are, tell me where Geordie is!"

"There isn't a feller called Geordie in these parts," murmured a sleepy voice. "The feller alongside me was taken bad through me havin' a game with 'im."

At the sound of the voice Dick shivered in the hot air and shrank away. He stared into the darkness, but his eyes might just as well have been shut.

"I knowed you too," the voice went on more drowsily still. "Just you stick your arm round my neck and I'll go off as sweet as heaven."

"Don't speak, only tell me where he is," whispered Dick.

"Climb over me then. You've no call to move your arm."

Dick felt himself trembling all over from the poison of the air. He had hardly strength to creep across the body, but close on the other side he found him for whom he was seeking. With a last effort he wound his right arm under the head, and laid his face beside it. "Haven't you a word left for me?" he whispered, and with the deep breath of a child going to sleep he stretched himself full length upon the motionless form of his comrade.

"Damn them furreigners!" cried Shadow, impatiently stamping the quick mark-time in the stable far away. "What's the good of 'em always workin' overtime and keepin' my poor 'osses from their comfortable 'ome? I can't see no call for furreigners myself, never could, neither French nor German, North nor Welsh, nor nothink. The Marshal will be fair bustin' with emptiness for his corn and drinks."

He listened from the door, and imitating a bugle, he sang the infantry kitchen-call, which all the ponies knew as well as German wild boars know the sound of the forester's potatoes pattering on the frozen earth. But no rumbling wheels answered; and taking his lamp, he set out in search, cursing the perversity of all the human race which was not born in Wenley.

Arrived at the black hole, he called again,

and a feeble whinny replied. He found that the Marshal had tried to back down into the air-way, but had got jammed athwart, and now stood quivering, whilst the sweat dripped from his sides. Shadow cut him loose, and he staggered slowly away, like one on whom the Fury has for a moment gazed and then passed on.

"My God, if it ain't the fire-stink!" said Shadow, ceasing to storm, and crouching close to the ground as he ran quickly forward. The "damp" was gradually rising again, and his lamp showed one little spark. Suddenly he stopped, and drew in his breath.

"Why, it's a perfect battlefield!" he said.

He felt the three bodies in turn. Two gave no sign, but Dick moaned.

"What, Dick, you dirty little devil!" cried Shadow. "Wake oop, can't yer, and coom along wi' me. Wake oop, you young cuss! Do ye know yer've pretty nigh killed the Marshal?"

"Take the other man," murmured Dick, "and leave me with my mate."

But Shadow had already uncoupled an empty tub and let down the side. One by one he dragged the bodies up, and shoved and lifted them into it. They lay there limp and jammed together like slaughtered carcases. By the time he had run the tub out of the working, Shadow himself was quivering and ready to drop. But pushing with all the strength left in him, he made his way towards the sump. The Marshal feebly ambled behind him with legs as unwarlike as a new-born lamb's.

"What's thee got there, Shadow?" said old Job, who was left alone at the foot of the shaft.

"I don't rightly know what to call 'em now," Shadow answered; "but two on 'em was Geordie and Dick, and t'other looks to me like the Kinestead unemployed as was took on yesterday. I told the Butty 'ow it 'ud be if he kep' on turnin' the old pit into a Casual Ward; and now they've gone and pretty nigh killed one of my 'osses!"

"Why, man alive! them's dyin' of the fire-stink," said old Job, peering into the tub, aghast.

"I'd ought to know that much for myself," said Shadow. "See me shakin'! Quick with it! We must damp 'em down now afore the fresh air carries 'em off. Here's two corn sacks for them two men. Lay hold, and I'll damp down Dick with his shirt and my old jacket."

They lapped the sacks tightly round the heads, and taking Dick's shirt, they turned it back over his face, old Job holding up a lamp.

"Oh, look 'e, Shadow—look 'e!" he cried. "Dick don't seem to be the kind of thing as he give 'imself out for!"

"O Job, Job, don't yer take no notice for what you see! you look the other way. Who'd 'ave thought such things could 'appen in the Trigger Pit? It is clean agen the Abstract of the Regulation Act for his Lordship's mines."

As Shadow spoke he was binding up Dick's head in his own jacket, and with trembling fingers was trying to button his own waistcoat round the naked body, and all the time he cried and sobbed, like a soldier who in the midst of a battle finds that he has driven his bayonet home between a woman's breasts.

They rang the signal four times, and then once more to show that men were coming up. At the top the miners, seeing the terrible load, came running out of the hovel where they were drinking their allowance of beer. The bodies were caught up and carried off to the engine-house.

"Gord's truth, her's a female!" cried the giant Manasseh, who had Dick in his arms.

At the word the miners gathered round, uttering the most complex oaths, and catching hold of her hands and feet, or trying to touch her grimy clothes, as though she had been a mediæval saint with power to stop a pestilence.

Hour after hour the bodies lay stretched out side by side in the engine-house. The doctor came. The whole village came. The black crowd stood in the snow, murmuring conjectures, though evening and night fell. At last there were sounds of moving and talking in the shed. Shadow appeared at the top of the steps swinging both arms as signals. The crowd hummed with expectation. A few minutes later Geordie and the Kinestead unemployed were seen being helped through the door. No one paid much attention to them. Behind them came the doctor, carrying Dick. All drew in their breath, and then the long cry of joy went up, and it was the women's turn to weep.

The doctor's own gig received the three,

and attended by all Wenley, it was slowly led to the doctor's own house. Patsy was kept there for the night, being too weakly to be moved. But when the other two were going home, he sat up in bed and made this little speech: "Look here, Richard Redford, if you want's my forgiveness for that little affair between us, you can take it and welcome, seein' it was all my own doin' through not fightin' you on the square. In place of drawin' my knife on you, I ought to have given you a oner low down in the ribs. It would have settled you almost as well as a knife. But I'm willin' to overlook my mistake as a bygone, and here's me hand on it. It isn't often a murthered ghost lives to ask his murtherer's pardon for the deed. But if you would want to fight me agin, you've only got to send me time and place, and you're welcome."

"Good-bye to ye, Madge," he went on, turning to Dick. "I will never go to sleep agin with your arm around me neck. So good-bye to you, me dear."

"Good-bye, Patsy dear," said Madge. "Nobody ever made me so happy as you've made me to-day, and nobody ever will."

Escaping with laughter and quick retorts from the inquisitive watchers in the street, Richard drew his marrow into their little cottage and locked the door. A blazing fire had been heaped up for them on the hearth. In front of it they stood enfolded in each other's arms.

"You may wash the black off me now, dear," said Madge, "just this once more. It has been a sweet, sweet time."

"Ay, you can say so now."

"Yes, for I have been all in all to you, as I shall never be again."

"But we are free—free to face the world together. And you shall be my marrow still; I love you so."

"Not a bit more than I love you," she said. "But you must find, another word for me than marrow now. Bone of the bone is well enough, but to be two together adds an endlessness to joy."

He lifted her up in his arms and carried her to and fro in the firelight like a little child. She laid her velvety little head upon his shoulder, laughing, and then sighing with the full contentment of hard-won peace.

"Dearest of men," she said, "you know what word you once asked me to call you. I will call you that now. But there is one thing we must do—we must send to your mother and all at Kinestead to tell them how clever we've been."

"Yes, yes," he said, "we'll send, but not to-night, not to-night."

"No, not to-night, my husband," she whispered, and in the silence of their chamber they could hear the great pit panting out the exhaust-air from the engine, like a beast disappointed of its prey.

But Miss Rachel was already lying, very neat and white, ten foot under the snow which lay on Kinestead churchyard as neat and white as she.

XII

AN OLD RED RAG

THE politics of the natives in Wenley had always been simple and steadfast, like their religion. As they hated the Pope by tradition, and the Devil by courtesy, so they touched their caps to the rich, and voted against the Radical. They were Conservative almost to a man; they did not exactly know why. To be anything else argued unnatural perversity, a mean and carping spirit. The very name of Tory had a rotund and substantial sound, genial as ale and beef. How meagre and peevish were the rival words, suggestive of schoolmasters, lawyers, nondescripts who write books, idlers who waste life in reading them, and other wry fellows of that sort—a sour and inhuman company, like a row of medicine bottles. But the Tory had humour and sweet blood. He clapped his hand on his pocket, and looked out upon life with the heart of a friend. He alone seemed to be a man; the rest flitted about like shades.

In the village itself a high standard of misery was always maintained; but misery had no influence on political opinion. Politics were a thing far removed above the dull level of common life. Politics were the proper theme for glowing eloquence beside the glowing bar; they were the one sure source of inspiring converse, the one fine vision of realms beyond the horizon of the dingy street. Every fifth year, or oftener, they afforded a spectacle of contest nearly equal to a football match or horse race, without the annoyance of gatemoney. Even woman, whom Nature for her own wise purposes had created incapable of politics as of sport—even woman could applaud the crushing argument of the victorious male, and crown him with her smile above the beer. Who, then, would degrade so fine an essence as politics to hew and draw for the squalid needs of home? Politics had no more connection with daily life than charity has with a modern philanthropist's dinner.

So daily life went on for better or worse,

and during this winter it went badly. For six weeks after the New Year the snow was deep, with hardly a break, and frost held Wenley in its grip. From the first the quarries had been silent, and the potteries shut soon after. The pits were only just kept going. On the canals along the valley the barges, loaded with coal and iron, lay enclosed in ice like Arctic ships. Trade was reduced to primeval barter. Piteous tales were whispered, and in the cupboard of each house stood a skeleton shamelessly exposed. The spoil-heaps at the pit's mouth were sifted again and again by tiny fingers searching for lumps of coal. Tiny forms shivered up and down the street with their irresistible cry of hunger, and one shawl now covered the heads of two.

But man's necessity is the director's opportunity. Accurate reports of the distress reached the distant offices of the Quarry Company. In the fourth week there were signs that the frost was breaking. Now was the time to make the heart of the shareholder throb with confidence in the directors; for what resistance can be looked for from men with hungry families? A notice appeared announcing a reduction of four shillings in the pound for all labourers in the "bloke-hole" or open quarry. Wenley stood aghast. Even the manager telegraphed a protest. The answer was, "Take it or leave it"—a message of less than sixpenny politeness.

To weeks of frost succeeded weeks of dismal strike, varied by frost and thaw. A spirit of bewildered and helpless anger began to brood over the village, and day by day vague murmurs and complaints increased. The climax came when a hard-working quarryman, the father of five children, started for the town one morning to look for work, and was found dead in a snowy ditch. He had given his breakfast of bread and dripping to the children. At the news his widow's milk dried up, and her baby died. Even Nature then was turning from her sweet uses and betraying the hearts who trusted her, and no one could say on whom the next blow might fall.

The following Sunday was fixed for the funeral of the quarryman and his shrivelled baby. A funeral was almost the only thing at Wenley which afforded those moments of intensified sensation so highly valued by modern thought, and the village inevitably looked forward to the spectacle with a pleasurable interest. But otherwise it was restless and uneasy that Saturday night, and in the morning it woke to find that a strange miracle had happened in the darkness. Under each door in the village lay a little printed paper, as surprising as heavenly food, though less satisfying. On one side was a set of verses, well known to have been composed, syllable by syllable, and elaborated almost to the scanning point, by the deceased quarryman during the literary leisure of those long weeks of "play" and starvation. On the other was an address to workers, in business-like prose, containing statements which seemed to turn the natural order of things wrong way up, like an earthquake. All morning the men stood at the house doors or corners of the streets, discussing it in disjointed words with long intervals of silence between. Now and then some one would pull out the address and read it aloud for the benefit of those whose wives had thriftily burnt it to help the little fires. It spoke of "capitalists" and the "proletariat" and other incomprehensible things which did not matter. But there was one intelligible sentence, and it said, "All wealth belongs to the workers." Now, that was a lie, and every sensible man knew the exact epithet by which that lie should be described. Wealth belonged to the rich, and they used it in giving employment, supporting charities, and otherwise enjoying themselves. Wenley had no doubts on that point, and after seeing so monstrous a statement put forth with all the pomp and authority of print, it was quite a relief to look down the street and behold the pigeons still flying about and the old earth still solid and unshaken.

At half-past three the funeral procession was formed up in front of the quarryman's cottage. By immemorial custom the baby's coffin was carried by four girls dressed in white, with white cotton gloves, and long white "falls" over their heads. When they came out bearing the little wooden thing by its handles between them, a strange sound rose from the crowd — a deep breath of pity and deadly interest, but a deeper sound beside. Behind the little child came the dead father; then the widow, held from falling by her brother, one of the Doggies at Number Nine Pit; then her four surviving children in line, arranged by height. The procession moved slowly up the hill, the people following it, and closing in upon the road. In front, a policeman cleared the way, patiently trying to persuade the children they would see both coffins quite plain if only they stood back.

At the lych-gate of the old churchyard on the hill-top, the parson stood waiting in his semi-transparent surplice, and his thin voice was heard beginning the service as the bearers approached. The hushed crowd passed through the entrance, and trampled the snow on the grave-mounds. Panting matrons still came hurrying up from washing the few plates after the starved Sunday dinner, and whispered to inattentive neighbours what a race they had had to overtake the funeral. At last it might have been thought that all Wenley had arrived.

But there was one away still. In his attic overlooking the churchyard old Karl Meyer, "the German," as he was called, sat with his elbows on the bare board of the table, and listened to the tramp of the people, and their voiceless murmur. His large dark eyes, wild with the light of ennobling illusions, were fixed as in a trance upon a red canvas flag, which was nailed to a rough stick and hung over the bed by a rusty hook. It was a faded old thing, stained by age, and pierced by three ugly holes; but except for a print of the massacre of the Communards in Père la Chaise, it was the only decoration upon the walls, from which the whitewash was blistering off in flakes, and as the old man gazed on it, the dull-red hue began to work in his brain, conjuring up strange visions of the past and future. He was an unknown artisan now, engaged day after day for a few shillings a week in moulding the crushed marl into shapes for drain-pipes, and people called him Carlo, because he was so good-tempered and so shaggy; but that red flag transported him to a very different scene of nearly fifty years ago. Then he was a young sculptor, with smooth pale face and brilliant eyes that women loved, and he dwelt far away in a beautiful old town, from the walls of which the jagged barrier of the Alps themselves could just be seen on sunny mornings in the spring. He seemed to feel once more the long and radiant months pass over him in their joyous course, whilst he lived among his fellows, devoted to his art, and to an inspiring new philosophy which was even now ushering in a new era of hope for all mankind. How they had all preached and plotted and sung—himself amongst the very leaders, young as he was! Did not their paper once write of him as the young Brutus of the Revolution? Then at last the day of days arrived, and the elated crowd—students, artists, and working-men, bound together by the passion for liberty—went sweeping through the streets to conquer for all humanity the rights of man, and Karl was at their very head. On he rushed, though in his front the volleys rang, and behind him the dead fell and the wounded shrieked. He gave no heed to them, for the sun was in his blood, and the joy of a cause which can never be crushed out. Armed only with his glorious red flag, he charged forward, ever forward, whilst the whole earth seemed to cheer him on, and the sky laughed for delight. Suddenly, as in a dream, the Royal Palace appeared just in front with its staring façade of white marble, and there were the soldiers drawn up in line, for their last stand, on each side of the central arch. Once and again they fired, but their volleys were ragged now. They hesitated, and looked behind them as if for orders. Then sullenly laying down their arms, they came with outstretched hands to meet the people. Mingled with the exultant crowd, almost torn to pieces by the caresses of the women, they were carried onward in a wild stream through the Palace gates. The King had abdicated and fled. The people then was King. From all the happy, seething multitude arose the triumphant shout of freedom, and Karl himself was hoisted on to the balustrade at the top of the marble steps, to wave the red flag as the signal of victory — a beacon signal of a new age risen at last for suffering mankind on that glorious morning nearly fifty years ago, when Karl and all the world were young.

"I say, comrade," said a rough voice behind him, and a round, good-humoured face was deferentially pushed in at the door, "you surely ain't goin' to miss the Revolution after all?"

It was Jock, "Lubber Jock," as he was called,

one of Karl's mates in the pottery, and the most faithful attendant at his discussions in the Economic Club, which Dr. Maguire had instituted on Saturday evenings, chiefly to occupy the excitable old man's mind, and divert it from empty brooding. The Club had now been at work for nearly a year, and it numbered four members.

"What Revolution?" cried Karl, starting up from his dream at the word, and turning sharply round to face his comrade in the cause.

"Why, our Revolution, to be sure," answered Jock, looking rather disconcerted, and shifting about from one foot to another, like a schoolboy before his master. "It's just the right time to have it now, and both the other fellows in the Club say so too—what with the funeral and the strike, and it bein' Sunday, and the people starvin'. And those bits of paper we give out last night, they've been and made a fine disturbance, I can tell you. Why, I'm fair sick of answerin' questions, and tellin' people as the bourgeois is such as call their parlour a drawin'-room."

Old Karl went to the window and looked out upon the dingy, shivering crowd in the churchyard. The service was nearly over. The coffins had been lowered out of sight, and the clergyman was sprinkling the symbolic grains of earth. The four white bearers at the corners of the grave looked like guardian angels, and at the sight of them the women were weeping without restraint, whilst the men stood moodily silent, turning their caps round and round for fear of displaying emotion ; but now and again they said "Amen," out of respect for the man who had given up his life for his children.

"Now's our time," said Jock. "Come along."

But Karl did not hear him. He was still gazing upon the crowd; and as he gazed, his eyes kindled with a strange light, such as was seen upon the face of him who stole fire from the rosy gods and brought it down to mortals shuddering in their glacial caves.

"O sons of men," he murmured, "too unhappy, did you but know your unhappiness! Yet I would that for one day you might know it, and see it as it is, the unending unhappiness of the poor—how insecure, uncertain of the morrow, full of vague apprehensions and forebodings, and terrified at every change, along the crumbling edge of the abyss we creep from day to day towards death, comforted by the one hope of finding him before we are helpless and can no longer toil. Nay, rather I would that for one day you might know how full and strong life can really be, that having enjoyed for one day the exercise of faculty, the wide knowledge, the calm security, and confident hope, claimed as mere necessaries by those before whom you hardly dare to open your mouths in fear of their undefined powers and advantages, you might become possessed by so noble a hunger for a noble life as could never be resisted or denied."

"Hunger?" said Jock. "They're 'ungry enough, you take my word. Anyways, if I was a bit of roast-meat, I wouldn't trust myself down there among 'em. Come along, old mate; now's our time, just before they start goin' home."

But Karl first turned and unhooked the red flag from over his bed, and rubbed the dust off upon the counterpane.

"Let me carry that," said Jock; "and I only wish I'd thought to drop on a bit of fresh glue first to 'old it tighter to the stick. But I'll treat it very careful."

AN OLD RED RAG

However, old Karl held the flag himself, and they sallied out together into the crowd. The people stood aside to let them pass, for everybody liked Carlo, and respected him as the steadiest of workmen and the most generous. It was true he was a foreigner, and was said to hold strong opinions. All foreigners did hold strong opinions; that was nature's compensation to them for their feebleness in other respects, and their ignorance of sport. But there was hardly a villager under thirty who did not owe him some pleasant memory of childhood; and all children regarded him as a sort of large Newfoundland dog, a kind old thing, created expressly for their amusement and delight.

What that red flag was for no one could understand, but they naturally connected it with the Salvation Army.

"No," Lubber Jock explained; "it ain't exackly the Army. It's the Revolution just begun—beggin' your pardon, miss, for trampin' on your feet."

When they had made their way to the middle of the churchyard, Karl climbed on to a flat tombstone beside the newly made grave. " My comrades in poverty," he cried, and at the sound of his voice all raised their faces towards the ditch-water sky in which a flock of rooks was wildly circling round, like stirred tea-leaves in a poor man's cup—"this little baby and its father have died of hunger. Now that the parson has gone home, there is not one among us here who does not know what hunger is. These two poor sons of man have died of it. They have now been put into the earth to rot because they had no food. They were our comrades. They have been killed at our side. If they had been killed in battle, should we leave them unavenged?" ("Never!" shouted a well-known military voice, and there was some laughter among the people.) "We are in battle. We are fighting the great battle of the poor. How long shall it last? How long shall it last before we strike our enemy? Injustice has been done us long enough." ("Injoostice! That's where it is! It's injoostice!" murmured the crowd.) "If we knew where the injustice lay, should we not take it by the throat? should we not run it through the heart?" ("For Queen and country!" cried the voice again.) "It is no good waiting for other people to do it for us. We must live our own life and fight our own battle. For every working-man imprisoned or killed for this cause, ten spring up in his place. These two comrades of ours, now covered up in the earth —do you think their life is ended? In our hearts their souls go marching along. They have already become a regiment of fighters. Let us then raise our protest in the face of the sun. People may laugh at it. They may damp it down. They may stamp it out. But in the end it reaches home. At the worst they can but kill us, and in this battle death does not count. As we go to fight this fresh battle in the eternal rebellion of the poor, let us raise the song which our dead comrade made to help us."

"To the tune of 'The Sweet By-and-by,'" cried Jock, springing up beside his hero. "It don't quite fit, but we must do as best we can."

Amid mingled cheers and questions and unwonted shouts of excitement, he led off with the now familiar words:

"All you that have hearts as can feel,
　　Pray show in kind pity your aid,
　In this our most earnest appeal—
　　We ask it of every trade.

"Necessity urges us on
　　To seek the protection of those
　Who can by their sympathy soothe
　　Our grief and lamentable woes.

"Our masters, still more to lament,
　　Instead of the pain to allay,
　They have come to a speedy consent
　　To drop us of fivepence a day."

Singing the remaining lines, and then beginning with the first verse over again, the crowd, with excited faces and bewildered cries of anger, swept in a confused mass out of the churchyard and down the village street. The policeman, though rather uncertain of his duty, marched in front, clearing the road for the Revolution, which he supposed, from the flag, might be perhaps, after all, only a new kind of Band of Hope. Behind him came the four members of the Economic Club, with Karl in the midst, his sad eyes fixed on visions. Was it not then just possible that on this dull day and in this dreary village it should really begin at last—that radiant time of universal hope? What if, after all, it should be his hand which was destined to lead it in? The wild singing, the shouts, and crowding of the people behind him filled his soul with a joyful madness. In all that noise he heard the voice of mankind risen at last against the immemorial wrongs which it had suffered and itself inflicted. Quick thoughts of struggle and of victory sped through his brain like fiery serpents, and vanished, leaving glad vistas of an earth transformed, a larger day, wherein there moved an equal and nobler breed of men through golden fields, on golden seas, under a golden sky.

On reaching the quarryman's deserted cottage, the crowd stopped by instinct and formed a lane, down which the widow passed in tears, whilst her flustered children walked huddled together behind her, in all the self-importance of children's mourning.

"God knows," she said at the door, "there's neither bite nor sup in the house, or I'd give it you all, and welcome, in return for the burying and kindness you've done me."

"Never you speak on it, Mrs. Smalley," said

Jock, taking off his cap to divert attention from his pity. "And I'm only thankful them as are gone have had a decent day for the funeral."

When the mournful family had disappeared into their home bereft, the people stood looking at Carlo and at each other, uncertain what was to be done next. "How about raisin' that there protest?" some asked.

"Why, haven't we just been and raised it?" answered the more contented, and many went off to their homes in the gathering darkness. Others began the quarryman's hymn again, or crowding round the red flag, waited for orders like soldiers anxious for the keen reality of battle. And with a soldier's instinct, mindful of old Bavarian training, Karl strove to arrange them roughly into "fours," like a regiment on the march, the other members of the Club assisting him as best they could, and endeavouring, though quite vainly, to keep the women and children in the place of safety at the centre.

At last they began to move slowly forward again along the road towards the quarries, Karl still bearing the flag at the head of the loose and straggling column. "We're goin' to raise that protest in the manager's front passage," they said. "We're goin' to arbitrate a bit." "The manager's got a heart. He knows what joostice is." "Wait till old Carlo speaks to him."

It seemed a practical proposal for the next step, and the next step is always the most important thing. Perhaps the directors might give way, and then the Revolution would be over, and everything go on as before. So on they marched, taking up another verse of the quarryman's hymn:

> "We cannot maintain by the drop
>   Our children, they know very well;
> And by their ambition, no doubt,
>   They will drive many thousands to hell."

But it so happened that the road led past the vicarage, a suitable home for an Anglican clergyman; for it stood in the midst of a nice garden enclosed by a high brick wall, and the entrance-porch was approached by a smooth carriage-drive. In summer the wistaria hung very prettily over the front of the house, and in the upper stories were plenty of bedrooms. The clergyman himself was a devoted servant of the English Church, intent on upholding the light of her comeliness and chastened dignity in the midst of a gross and unbeautiful land. No one could doubt his zeal for her services, and in ruri-diaconal conferences his voice carried weight upon questions of historic use. But in the village itself he had always been confronted by a good-tempered tolerance, which he would very willingly have exchanged for open scorn and persecution. For nature had endowed him with a martyr spirit, and in face of the peaceful but steady indifference of his flock almost the only consolation left for him was to cherish the emptiness of his church on Sundays, very much as martyrs on stained glass windows are represented cherishing the instruments of their martyrdom.

As the marshalled crowd was approaching the vicarage gates, there came a pause in their singing, and a voice in front cried out: "Why not call on parson and get something out of him? Who says?"

The proposal was greeted with a shout of laughing assent.

"None of that!" cried Jock angrily. "Parson's got nothing to do with we, and I'm sorry for him besides."

"Why, Jock," some one expostulated, "you ain't got no cause to be sorry for him. He's no better than a blank Cartholic."

"It ain't of his choir I'm thinkin', nor yet of his petticoats, but I'm sorry for him," replied Jock stubbornly.

"They tell me he draws eight pound a week," shouted the collier who had first made the proposal. "That's pretty nigh ten times more nor me, and all I'm offerin' is to change jobs with him—him to do my work in the pit, and me to take on his job for just half his money. That's fair, ain't it?"

"Brayvo, parson Uriah!" laughed the people.

"It ain't his money I'm thinkin' on neither, nor yet his doin' no work," said Jock; "but I'm sorry for him."

But expostulation was in vain. Carlo himself had stopped, and was turning towards the house. "Let me alone, comrade," he cried, shaking Jock's hand from his shoulder. "The people are right. The priests shall be the first to feel the coming overthrow. Too long have they held the people bound in ignorance at the feet of the possessing classes, whilst from their comfortable homes they preach contentment to the poor. Too long has their incense-smoke darkened the sun, and their wealth mocked at their praise of poverty. 'Behold I come again to be crucified,' said the man who centuries ago foresaw the world of to-day; for now indeed the son of man is crucified afresh, and the priests look on, telling him that if only he were more like them his cross would give no pain."

"I don't know anything about that, old man," said Jock; "but you'll never do no good raisin' a protest to parson. We ain't no concern of his. Besides, I'm sorry for him, he's done that bad with his pigs. Two on 'em's just died of the frost, and one was near fat enough for killin'."

But the folding gates had already been thrown open, and the crowd swarmed in upon the ecclesiastical property, and stood gaping up at the vicarage windows, as the Vandals gaped on Rome.

The vicar was finishing off his evening sermon on the hunger and thirst after righteousness. His wife and five of the children were still at tea, whilst the youngest was being put to bed upstairs. Seeing the people trooping into the garden, the children at the tea-table at once jumped up, and whitened their noses against the window-panes, wondering why it was the carol-singers had come again, now that Christmas was over. For, drawn up in rough lines in front of the house, the Revolutionists began singing what seemed to them the most appropriate verse of their hymn :

> "O heavenly Father above,
> Protect us, we heartily crave;
> For surely our masters intend
> To hurry us into the grave."

Unfortunately it happened that the vicar kept an enthusiastic gardener, steeped in the Conservatism which gardening naturally diffuses. He had followed the course of the Revolution from the beginning with smouldering wrath, and now he was compelled to view the rioters actually invading his own dear province. Possessed by the rage of property, he hastily caught up an old loaded vermin-killer, and ran into the house to take up a fortified position behind the parapet over the porch. Before the hymn was well over, he appeared, gun in hand, and shouted to the people : " Look here, you there ! You just come off them flower-beds, and stop tramplin' on my bulbs!"

"Bulbs!" laughed the crowd in derision. "Hark to him! Bulbs! and we's starvin'!"

Very slowly the gardener raised his gun. "You get off them snowdrops," he said, "or I'll fire."

"Surely he ain't never goin' to shoot at we!" whispered one or two women, drawing their children behind them.

"Never mind for him," Jock called out cheerily. "He's only havin' a bit of a game."

But Carlo sprang to the front door, scattered its glass panels with a violent crash, and broke through into the passage. No one heeded him any more, for at that moment a round jet of orange flame spouted from the thin barrel on which all eyes were fixed. The report was hardly heard. Instantly a young girl at the back of the crowd began to shriek with pain and terror. A shot had grazed her hair, and drawn a tiny drop of blood.

No one could ever say how it all happened, but with a wild outcry of fury the people found themselves surging up against the walls of the house, and hanging there for a while, like a wave driven against a barrier. Then through every opening they flowed into all the rooms and passages, and stood staring at each other, and at the walls and furniture, bewildered and rather alarmed by so unusual a situation.

In the dining-room the vicar's family had disappeared; but the tea-things were left standing on the table, the cups half empty, and the hungry people looked at them sideways, and seemed to hesitate as they entered the room, walking rather carefully for fear of spoiling the carpet with their boots. But one young mother, being already outside the law, did not hesitate. Sitting by the urn in the place of the vicar's wife, she hastily began feeding her child with anything that came to hand.

"You're makin' free, young woman," said the others.

"Don't care. He's 'ungry," was the answer.

"Well, if that's all," said a matron in her own right, "I s'pose it's Christianity, and they do say parson's a Christian."

It seemed a valid argument, and the dining-room soon wore the air of a spirited mothers' meeting, with provisions thrown in.

Meantime the rest of the house was rapidly

filling, as the people crowded into the kitchens and swarmed upstairs. With every step their fury died away. The strike, the protest, even their hunger, were almost forgotten in the interest and excitement of the moment. Like children in a fairy-land, they passed from room to room, admiring everything, fingering everything—the polished dish-covers, the lots of utensils needed to cook a parson's dinner, the shining rows of various plates—enough to feed a bishop, one would have thought. To make a climax of amusement, the three maid-servants were discovered hidden away in the coal-cellar, and actually in tears; so terrified at their own friends and relations, that they had to be comforted by glorious laughter, and the masculine endearments which reassure the heart.

Upstairs, tall looking-glasses reflected unwonted forms, unwonted attitudes. Beds were turned down, sheets and quilts stroked with many exclamations of wonder. Children discovered the miracle of the bell-handles, and soon a merry peal was ringing. They shut each other up in wardrobes, and improvised a lordly hide-and-seek up and down the back stairs. But, after all, the drawing-room was the true centre of joy. There the women almost spoke in whispers, pointing out with reverence the gold of the picture-frames, the flowery chintz covers, the rows of gilded books, the profound arm-chairs, the brass fender, the banner-screen of the vicar's college arms worked in coloured wools. The whole scene was soon converted into one wild revel of amiable delight. Perhaps it was the only really successful conversazione or "At Home" which has ever been held for working people.

The vicar, in his remote study at the top of the house, gradually became aware of an irritating disturbance. He paused in the midst of his peroration, inwardly expressing his annoyance by a phrase too hastily borrowed from the Athanasian Creed. At length, laying down his pen in despair, he opened the door to listen, and was at once confronted by the benign form of Lubber Jock.

"Beg pardon, I'm sure, sir, for interruptin' of you," said the English sans-culotte; "but it'll be best for you to stop where you be till the Revolution's over, and I thought I'd come and tell you, because I've said all along I was sorry for you."

"Revolution, my good fellow! You sorry for *me!* Why—what does all this mean? Stand aside at once."

"No, sir, none of that! You don't come out. Now, don't you be drivin' me to do nothing rash. I'm pretty nigh twice your fightin' weight. But I'm sorry for you."

"Stand aside, fellow, and let me pass! There's the bell beginning for service."

"Beg pardon, I'm sure, sir," said Jock, forcing him very gently back into the study, and locking the door on the outside; "but I'm goin' to keep you safe, because I'm sorry for you. Service'll have to dally till the Revolution's over."

Disregarding the vicar's liturgy of appeal from behind the door, Jock pocketed the key, and returned, peacefully smiling, to the cheerful scene downstairs. At the moment there was a pause in the festivity. The pleased and interested people were looking round for the next "event" on the unconsidered programme, and some of the women, mindful of household duties, were already saying good-night, when suddenly from some distant part of the house a cry arose: "The police, the police!"

It was caught up on all sides. The police had been seen swarming in. The military had been called out. A whole regiment of red-coats was scrambling though the scullery window—a poor barrier against love at all events, as some of the men knew well, and possibly a poor barrier against law. The people stood still and looked at each other with dismayed faces. "The police!" "The soldiers!" Still the cries came. The inveterate habit of law renewed its hold upon the victims of injustice, and their hearts failed under poverty's terrors. They began in knots to struggle out of the kitchen and force their way along the passages. It was surely useless for one to stand whilst others were escaping. Man after man yielded to the infection of panic, and the front door was soon jammed by a shouting and struggling crowd, tearing at each other in their desire only to get outside once more and breathe the free air of night.

But the leader of the Revolution was far away in an upper storey pursuing a relentless search for the man who had fired on the crowd. That shot had added flame to the accumulated store of indefinite hatred within him, and like an avenging hound of fate he had sought the trace of the offender from covert to covert through all rooms and lurking-places. On a landing over the porch he had found the old gun still smoking from one barrel, and on his quest he carried it in his right hand ready for vengeance. Just as he had entered the nursery in its turn, he heard the loud outcries of "Police!" from downstairs, and recognised the meaning of the sounds of rush and panic along the passages. Unwillingly he broke off his search, and listened. He recognised at once that a greater need than mere vengeance called him away, for now was the time to rally the people, and confront the agents of oppression with the first blow for a victorious cause. Tightening his grasp round the small of the gun, he strode to the door, but just as he reached it he heard a faint cry wailing through the deserted room—"O mother, mother, why ever don't you come?"

He stopped and looked round, for the voice was close at hand, but the place seemed empty. Again the cry came—"I want my mother;" and stooping down he perceived a terrified little face just peeping from under the valence of one of the beds.

"Where's my mother?" it wailed, at sight of Karl's alarming figure, and then withdrew under cover again.

"Why, what's the matter, my dear?" said he, going back and gently drawing a half-naked little figure from under the bed.

"I want my mother," it repeated and wailed louder than ever. It was the vicar's youngest child, left there half washed by the nurse when she fled. For refuge it had crept under the cot, clasping a favourite doll for protection to its heart.

"Never you mind, my dear, you'll be all right. Old Carlo will take you to your mother," said the Revolutionist, wrapping the naked little limbs for covering and warmth in the red flag, which he hastily tore from its pole. "Now put your head comfortable against my shoulder, and we'll go and look for her."

Easily reassured by his voice, and glad to escape from the twilight solitude of her hiding-place, the child laid one arm round Karl's neck, and with the other pushed his rough beard away from her face. So holding her tightly with his left hand, and still grasping the gun in his right, Karl ran hurriedly into the passage and down the flights of stairs, whispering as he ran all the soothing words he could remember from his own distant childhood in the forests, and between whiles shouting to the Revolutionists to stand firm.

But by the time he came in sight of the entrance-hall, the whole position had been abandoned, and was already occupied by the full armed forces of the plutocracy. These consisted of three policemen, and a militia recruit who had just returned from depôt for his first day's leave. The police had drawn their truncheons. The recruit was armed only with scarlet and prestige. Through the front door the last of the rioters was just disappearing, though Jock still stood there, trying in vain to muster them to an assault with one of the vicar's walking-sticks.

At the sight of Karl upon the stairs, the police-sergeant cried with scorn, " Here's the furreigner what makes the speeches! He's our man. Lay hold on that gun quick. You can never know but what he mightn't take a shot at we. And what's that red bundle as he's got?

Why, confound me, if he isn't runnin' off with one of the parson's children!"

But in Karl's eyes those four simple men, drawn up across his path, stood for the embodiment of the powers which from age to age had flayed and ground and brutalised the people. Single-handed though he was, he felt a great throb of joy at the thought that now at last he had them face to face, and could strike once more at that long tyranny. For years of hope deferred and disappointed life, in bitter loneliness and degradation, he had brooded over the chance of this moment's coming, and with a flush of pleasure he sprang forward, lifting the butt of the gun ready for the blow. But the fate which waits on Promethean rebels was waiting too for him. Hampered by the child, he could not even strike, and as he rushed forward to meet Jock, who was striving to creat a diversion in the enemy's rear, three truncheons fell pitilessly on his old grey head. It was the end of the Revolution in Wenley. Staggering forward for a few steps without a cry, he rolled in a heap on the door-mat. In falling he held out the child to Jock, that it might not be hurt.

"Looks as if you'd damaged old Carlo," said the recruit, stooping over him, and feeling very uncomfortable at the sight of the dark blood slowly trickling round the vicar's umbrella-stand.

"I only 'ope we've give him a good thrapin', I do," retorted the sergeant of police. "Furreigner, indeed! I'll learn him to be a furreigner!"

Whilst he spoke he was gently raising the grey head, and trying to make out where the hurt was, as he stanched the blood with his pocket-handkerchief. Almost too sick to stand, the scarlet recruit tottered off for the doctor.

When Doctor Maguire arrived, he found the prisoner still stretched upon the mat on which the people had so carefully wiped their boots. His head was supported upon the knees of the vicar's wife, whilst the child clung round her neck, wondering why an old man should be petted and nursed. On one side Jock knelt, sobbing in loud gasps, and suggesting useless remedies. On the other the police were drawn up in a sympathetic row.

"My old comrade," said the doctor, kneeling down, "why—why are you here?"

"Comrade," answered the dying man, "why are not you?"

Then as they were busy with unavailing bandages, and tried to lift him up and carry him away, "Let me be, let me be," he murmured. "It is nice and sunny here. Der Mai ist gekommen, die Blumen ziehen aus."

It was the beginning of an old song which the students in German universities sing about the streets on the first of May; and whilst he was trying to remember the tune, he died.

He was buried, as became a Communist, by the Commune—that is to say, the Parish; and the flag, after hanging for a time over the child's cot "as a memorial of her escape," was put in the fire by the housemaid, because it was really too dirty for anything. Beyond a few scornful or moralising articles in the newspapers, little notice was taken of the Revolution by the outside world, and by the time that summer came, everything seemed to be going on much as before at Wenley-on-the-Hill. Yet it would be untrue to say that even that old red rag had been woven in vain. For at times, when the myth of old Carlo was repeated beside the bar or at the corners of the streets, the minds of the listening groups would seem to kindle into a vivifying glow, red as the flag itself; but whether with sympathy only or with a desperate hope, even they would have found it hard to decide.

THE END

Printed by BALLANTYNE, HANSON & CO.
Edinburgh and London.

www.ingramcontent.com/pod-product-compliance
Lightning Source LLC
Chambersburg PA
CBHW031334230426
43670CB00006B/339